GOD
DOES NOT
FORECLOSE

GOD
DOES NOT
FORECLOSE

The Universal Promise of Salvation

DAVID LOWES WATSON

ABINGDON PRESS

Nashville

GOD DOES NOT FORECLOSE:
The Universal Promise of Salvation

This book is printed on acid-free paper.

Library of Congress Cataloging-in-Publication Data
Watson, David Lowes
   God does not foreclose : the universal promise of salvation /
David Lowes Watson.
      p.   cm.
   Includes bibliographical references and index.
   ISBN 0-687-14964-9 (alk. paper)
      1. Church renewal—United States.   2. Christianity and culture.
3. Mission of the church.   I. Title.
BR526.W32   1990
262'.001'7—dc20   90-36893
                                                                          CIP

MANUFACTURED IN THE UNITED STATES OF AMERICA

ACKNOWLEDGMENTS

I am grateful for the invitations to present lectures, in the preparation of which the chapters of this book were brought into focus: the Jackson Lectures at Perkins School of Theology, Southern Methodist University, Dallas, Texas; the Methodist Institute Lecture at Garrett-Evangelical Theological Seminary, Evanston, Illinois; the Trott Lectures at Wesley Theological Seminary, Washington, D.C.; and a Convocation on Evangelism at Eden Theological Seminary, St. Louis, Missouri.

I am also grateful to colleagues throughout The United Methodist Church who have heard these themes preached at Annual Conferences or Pastors' Schools. The stimulating dialogue which has ensued on each occasion has been a further encouragement to hone the material for publication.

The section in chapter 4 on the resurrection of Jesus owes much to my wrestling with the biblical texts in a set of homiletical resources for *Quarterly Review* (spring 1985); the discussion of Protestant anthropocentrism in chapter 5 is drawn from a paper presented to the Methodist Bicentennial Theological Consultation held at Candler School of Theology in 1983, subsequently published in *Wesleyan Theology Today*, edited by Theodore Runyon (Kingswood, 1985); and I first explored the particularity of Christian identity (chapter 6) in an article for *Missiology* (October 1984), which also appeared in *Conflict and Context*, edited by Mark Lau Branson and C. René Padilla (Eerdmans, 1986).

To serve with the General Board of Discipleship of The United Methodist Church means constant challenge from the critical issues facing North American Christians today. I remain grateful to my colleagues at the Board for this environment, especially to Ezra Earl Jones, the General Secretary. At Abingdon Press, Neil M. Alexander and Paul Franklyn have been unfailingly helpful and supportive of the project, and have given valuable advice in guiding it toward fulfillment. My thanks are also due Steven W. Cox for his careful preparation of the manuscript.

In holding the tension between gospel vision and faithful discipleship, I owe a tremendous debt to two Christian laymen, both of them mentors and fellow pilgrims in the faith: Ernest H. Teagle, whose commitment to theology constantly guards against thoughtless discipleship; and Robert B. O'Neal, whose commitment to discipleship constantly guards against theological procrastination. They leave me and many others in no doubt at all that we serve a risen Christ, and they will recognize much in the pages that follow.

Nashville
January 1990

C O N T E N T S

Chapter Five: Salvation and Discipleship: A Necessary Distinction.. 97

Chapter Six: Congregations and Disciples: Questions of Identity... 115

Conclusion: Christ-Centered Congregations........................... 136

A MAJOR ECCLESIAL BLOCKAGE

An Old Error

This book intends to make a minor contribution toward the clearing of a major blockage in the North American church.[1] Like many such blockages, this one is more extensive than it appears, and is certainly far more serious than might be inferred from the scant acknowledgment it receives in the pastoral agenda of most congregations. It has been caused by an old error: the misappropriation of God's grace as a particular benefit for Christians rather than a universal gift to be shared with the world. What in fact is the pouring out of God's love through Jesus Christ on the whole of humankind has come to be viewed as the privileged possession of some. Instead of channels of grace, congregations have come to be viewed as Christic health spas, where needy, but sensible, people may come to soothe their earthly discomforts and heighten their spiritual well-being.

It is of course one of the great mysteries of all time that God should have assigned to a particular people the announcement of universal salvation in Jesus Christ. In the well-known words of Alfred Loisy, "Jesus foretold the kingdom, and it was the Church that came."[2] Moreover, assigning such a universal responsibility was bound to be fraught with risk. For instead of accepting the servant role of messenger, there was always the possibility that the church would assume a proprietary role, and become jealous of a privileged status it was never meant to enjoy.

It is the premise of what follows that this is exactly what has happened in the North American church of today. Not that it is the first

9

time that servants of God have inflated their status. It happened with the Israelites more than once; it has happened perennially in the church across the centuries; and whenever it does happen, whenever the people of God lose sight of their universal commission, the grace of the gospel is seriously impeded.

Cultural Tensions

The reason for this is our own day and age is the same as in previous ecclesial generations: the struggle with the tensions of enculturation. These are different from those of *in*culturation, the adjustments the church must always make to its sociohistorical setting in order to communicate the gospel as a meaningful and relevant message.[3] *En*culturation, by contrast, is when the church succumbs to its sociocultural environment, as it has today in the United States. The hedonism, the individualism, and the bankruptcy of communal life in contemporary Western culture have all made their inroads into the identity of the North American church. In many instances, pastoral leaders have been co-opted quite directly into a cultic priesthood, which spends much of its time creating surrogate communities to fill the vacuums of numerous social impoverishments. Likewise, many congregations have followed their pastoral leaders, and allowed their identity to be shaped by the same cultural demands—as in the survey conducted by a major city newspaper several years ago, which rated the largest churches in town according to how well their singles classes afforded the opportunity of finding a good partner, or even a good date.

Gospel Pressures

At such times of enculturation, the gospel of Jesus Christ builds up pressure, and eventually bursts out of its social and ecclesial compounds. We are close now to such a time, and some of our best thinkers have given us ample warning. Jürgen Moltmann, for example, has pointed us to the spiritual potential of the church.[4] Frederick Herzog has defined the character of a church committed to justice.[5] Howard Snyder has indicated ways in which spiritual renewal reshapes the church.[6] And Leonardo Boff has gone so far as to identify an *ecclesiogenesis* among the base communities of Latin America.[7] Each of these authors makes clear that the priority of Christian discipleship is not the church *per se,* but the gospel of God's salvation in Jesus Christ.

When this message of Good News is faithfully received by Christians and handed over to the world—the "traditioning" of the gospel—then the ministry and mission of the church is clear. But when Christians fail to do this, and tradition the Good News primarily for themselves, to the neglect of its importance for the world, then the gospel builds up pressure and bursts forth, ecclesial dismay notwithstanding.

There are many examples of this gospel "explosion" throughout the two thousand years of church history; but the precedent was set at the Apostolic Conference (Acts 15; Gal. 2). The issue then was every bit as weighty as it is today. Was the gospel of Jesus Christ a universal message, or was it merely another prophecy for the Jews? Put differently, did one have to become a Jew in order to become a Christian?

Without demeaning the law in any way, Paul declared that the gospel could not be contained in the Jewish tradition. It could only be handed on to the world *through* the Jewish tradition. For the man, Jesus of Nazareth—born of a Jewish mother, suckled at a Jewish breast, weaned on Jewish food, nurtured by Jewish parents, who breathed the air of Galilee and fished in its waters, who walked the dusty roads of Palestine and sweated Jewish sweat, who mingled with the people, and especially with the outcasts—proclaimed and embodied the Good News that the God who was, and is, and is to be, is above all a saving God, a God who is righteous *because* of this saving nature. What is more, this Jew, who was done in by the institutional religionists of the day, was raised from the dead, and became the forerunner of a new humanity.

This was Good News such as could never be contained in a single religious tradition, distinctive and indispensable though that tradition might be. Therefore, argued Paul, either the tradition opens up to accept the power of this message and let it through to all the world, or the grace of God will break open the tradition, and if need be, bypass it altogether. Had Paul not forced this issue, we would not have the church today, but in all probability another minor Jewish sect. We would be living not in an inaugurated reign of God, but a mythical one. We would be able to view our planet not in the light of God's universal grace, as befits the first generation of humanity ever to see it photographed from outer space, but only with the myopia of sectarian religionists who have neither the good sense, nor the good breeding, to see that their election is not for privilege, but for purpose.

Crisis of Confidence

The grounds for suggesting that the North American church finds itself confronted with this same issue today are what might best be described as the symptoms of a middle-age crisis of confidence. We know the signs of such crises in persons, but they are just as clear in institutions like the church: the serious questioning of all that has happened hitherto; and the persistent, nagging possibility that much of what we have done thus far has been a terrible mistake. Instead of accepting the maturity of middle age, with all the benefits that might be shared with younger churches, unfavorable comparisons are drawn, with the implication that if only North American congregations could rediscover their enthusiasm for the gospel, they would emulate and even outdo their rapidly growing sister churches elsewhere in the world.

The result of this is a deep ecclesial introspection that leaves little room for the gospel to permeate the church, still less to flow through to the world. Thus the pressure is building for an explosion of grace which could well bypass the North American church, and render it, across the full theological spectrum from left to right, the best programmed, best monied, best propertied, best equipped, and best pastored backwater of the coming reign of God.

Unless, that is, we can clear the ecclesial blockage. There is still time to do so. It is not yet midnight. The wedding feast has not yet begun, and we can still trim our lamps (Matt. 25:1-13). But first, those of us in the North American church must recognize our ecclesial impediments, and remove them. We must accept that our view of the gospel is all too often sectarian—a gospel for some, but not for others. We must ask whether our churchly demeanor curtails the scope of God's grace, and thereby devalues the rich contributions to the coming reign of God from those who are not Christian. And we must also ask how often we busy ourselves with every imaginable tactic to attract people to our sphere of ecclesial activity and influence, be it intellectual stimulation, the meeting of social or personal needs, the fostering of community—anything, in fact, but a clear and direct statement of the gospel as a message of Good News.

Defective Traditioning

Indeed, there is no more incriminating evidence of our present ecclesial blockage than the widespread lack of confidence in the gospel to be found today, regardless of theological persuasion. Those of us who strive to win people for Christ often practice our evangelism as if we do not trust the gospel to do its work in God's good time by God's good grace. By the same token, those of us who prefer a less direct form of evangelism extol the implications of the gospel, both personal and social, yet will not trust the gospel *per se* to accomplish these results. In either case, we fall prey to the technics of an age that, as Jacques Ellul warned us forty years ago, would become fascinated with method for its own sake.[8] As a result, we disempower our members, who, sensing that they belong to a church that claims to have good news but does not find it particularly newsworthy, are quite understandably at a loss about what is their role as Christians in the world.

The reason for this extensive lack of confidence in the gospel, and the concomitant blockage of grace in the church, is a deficiency in our traditioning, both in how we receive the message of Good News, and in how we hand it over to the world. Too often we depreciate the unique efficacy of the cross in realizing our salvation; or else we diminish the scope of God's grace, which extends this salvation to all. The Good News of the gospel is that both of these pronouncements are profoundly true. Jesus suffered and died for the salvation of every human being, and it is God's will that not one of them be lost.

Universalist Polemics

When it comes to a faithful traditioning of this gospel in its fullness, however, and the implication that God's will might actually prevail, that all of humanity might one day be back home where they belong, there are those who immediately object. Their concern is that we must at all costs avoid universalism—the assumption that this global homecoming is already a reality. Indeed, in some quarters of the church, any use of the word "universal" in conjunction with the gospel seems guaranteed to engender soteriological dispute.[9]

One reason for this is that more of us in the North American church than would care to admit, given our present preoccupation with membership statistics, hold to a concept of salvation which states that only if a person accepts Jesus Christ by intentional decision will there be the prospect of eternal life. Only those who can claim to *be* saved are those who *are* saved. As for the rest? Well, the argument continues, we can't answer for them. But there's plenty of biblical evidence to show that if they refuse to accept the gospel, and continue to be unforgiven sinners, the best they can expect is eternal death, and at worst eternal punishment. We will leave it to God to work out the details, but we do know it will be something very nasty indeed. Once again, we rarely state it quite like that—but we do not disbelieve it.

Universal Hope

A great many church members are profoundly uncomfortable with such propositions. They conflict with the image of a loving God, and they do not ring true when we consider our friends and neighbors, who may not come to church, but who are good, decent people, with much to commend them in light of Jesus' teachings. Besides which, as Carl Braaten has argued, the appropriate attitude for Christians must be one of universal hope.[10] Although we can in no way predetermine the final outcome of Christ's saving work, or in any way tell God what to do, we can surely hope that God will manage to bring together the human family in its entirety to celebrate the heavenly feast. If the central truth of the gospel is that Jesus died for all the human race, then, to change metaphors, why is there such concern to close the game before the bottom of the ninth?[11]

We shall examine the scriptural referents for this eschatological hope in some detail. Not only will we find the evidence for it overwhelming, but we shall also find that there are severe biblical warnings against assuming that the church has a monopoly on God's grace. Nothing could be farther from the truth. Indeed, so far removed is it, that countless church members find this churchly possessiveness sufficiently puzzling, and even objectionable, as to hesitate to reach out with the gospel on such grounds. After all, it is not only our neighborly pagan who can perceive the unreasonableness of placing exclusive trust in the friendly local church representative for compass-headings to eternity. There are many Christians who see the issue in precisely the same light.

Soteriological Chauvinism

A universal hope does not permit us to deny that the fullness of God's grace was manifested in Jesus Christ. But we should resist the implication that Christians are the extent of God's salvific repertoire. There is a soteriological chauvinism in assuming that only through the witness of Christians, albeit faithful Christians, can God's salvation be extended to the human race. It is inconsistent with a God of grace to suggest that the eternal life or death of other human beings could ever depend on their response to particular expressions of the gospel message by particular persons at particular times, all of which are subject to the accidents of history.

Questions of Identity

But if forgiveness, reconciliation with God, and eternal life in and through Jesus Christ, are not the exclusive benefits of the Christian community, then what is the nature and purpose of the church? And if God's grace is not limited to Christians, then what does it mean to be a disciple? Many faithful church members are asking these questions, even if they are not voicing them. The North American church may be in a crisis of introspection; but the indications are that if its ecclesial blockage can be cleared, it could well enter into its prime of life as a servant of God.

Questions of Context

It will already be clear that the focus of our study is the church in the United States of America (described throughout as the North American church in order to distinguish it from that of Latin America, and likewise the church in Canada). As we proceed it will also be clear that our focus is on the predominantly Caucasian middle-class constituency of the church.

The purpose of such a focus is not to suggest that the strengths, weaknesses, pitfalls, and opportunities we shall discuss are necessarily unique to white North American Christians, but rather to avoid the implication that ecclesial issues in the United States are by definition those of the world church. Christians from other cultures, including those within the United States, may find some familiar problems and hopes in our investigations, but they are the ones to draw these inferences for themselves.

By the same token, there are features of the North American ecclesial task common to all Christians. Indeed, the recognition and recovery of these in distinction from the social context of the United States—what might be termed the "de-culturation" of the church—is a growing concern of a number of writers whose guidance we have come to respect in assessing our churchly life and work. A good example is the recent volume by Stanley Hauerwas and William H. Willimon, *Resident Aliens: Life in the Christian Colony.*[12] Christians are "colonizers" of the world, the authors argue, and are driven by the teachings of Jesus to a "completely new conception of what it means . . . to live with one another. That completely new conception is the church . . . [a] colony made up of those who are special, different, alien, and distinctive . . . formed by hearing [Jesus'] invitation and saying yes." The task of the church, therefore, is so to order our life in the colony that the world might look at us and know that God is busy redeeming humanity.[13]

Yet, for one who writes with the secular identity of resident alien in the United States, who has chosen to live in this country and has been graciously and warmly welcomed, another analogy comes to mind. Though in one sense Christians do have an identity over against this present world order, being privileged to know of the coming reign of God, to share in a foretaste of it, and to be entrusted with announcing and witnessing to it, yet in another sense we are no different at all. For *no one* belongs to the world as it is. The whole of humanity rather belongs to the world as it *will be*, under the rule of Christ Jesus.

In this other sense, therefore, Christians are not colonists, but true patriots—those who have joined Christ in waging the struggle for independence and liberation from the principalities and powers of this present world order.[14] There are others engaged in the struggle, whether or not they have officially signed up with Christ. There are many more whose participation is less than wholehearted, and whose commitment to the cause will tend to be withheld until the final outcome is known. But no one is excused from the effects of the struggle—and the citizenship of everyone in this new state is ensured nonetheless. For we shall all participate fully one day in its vision and its reality.

Those of us engaged in the struggle must be ready, therefore, not only for sacrificial service, but also for the final victory of Christ, when all people will claim their heritage, irrespective of their commitment or participation. And if this strikes us from time to time as an unduly frustrating role, let us never forget that the final victory will engulf any such resentments in a cosmic outbreak of joy, as the rest of creation applauds the fullness of God's salvation.

In the meantime, we must accept the identity of what J. C. Hoekendijk has called "the church inside out."[15] There is no part of the body of Christ with greater potential for this identity than the North American church; but first, we must open ourselves anew to the grace of God. And in our present cultural environment, this requires a radical realignment of our Christian discipleship, and a radical expansion of our view of God's salvation.

THE NORTH AMERICAN DILEMMA

The Need for Candor

Since much of what follows involves the clarification of Christian discipleship, it will be as well at the outset to establish a criterion of candor. For the key to Christian discipleship—the real thing, that is—is the childlike trust Jesus requires of those who accept his invitation to this way of life. The first disciples sent out in his name were warned to be as wise as serpents and as gentle as doves (Matt. 10:16); but they were given a little child as their role model (Matt. 18:1-5; Luke 9:46-48). Those whom Christ calls today must be no less trusting.

This maxim of childlike trust is simple but by no means simplistic, as is sometimes mistakenly inferred. For little children, among their many distinctive characteristics, are impulsively honest. In the well-known story, it was a little child who first had the temerity to declare that the emperor had no clothes. And time after time, as we can all recall from personal experience, it is a little child who will expose our adult deviousness with the innocent observation that things really are the way they are.

So it is with the Christian disciple, who is sent by Christ with the simple, truthful message that the world needs to be healed, and that God has done and is doing something about it. In the life, death, and resurrection of Jesus of Nazareth, God has joined the human race, in all our sin, suffering, and pain, to open up a new life for us and for the whole of planet Earth. As this new life unfolds in the presence and power of the Holy Spirit, the fullness of God's healing salvation is seen to be nothing less than heaven on earth—time and eternity fused in the *shalom* of universal peace, love, and justice, now and forever.

People cannot hear this Good News *as* good news until first they have accepted the bad news. Before the prognosis must come the diagnosis—that the world is desperately sick. A great deal of this sickness can be attributed to human sin; but there is much more wrong with planet Earth than human beings could have devised, even with the ingenuity of sin in all its shapes and forms. There is evil in the world; there is disease; there is pain and suffering; and all of this is far beyond the scope of human deeds or human neglect. It is a deep, deep mystery, and must remain so until the secrets of eternity are revealed. But the Christian disciple knows, and is commissioned to declare, that God intends all of the sickness to be healed. In Christ Jesus, hope has been brought to the world, and nothing short of a new creation shall come to pass, in which humanity will be reconciled with God, and the whole of planet Earth be restored to its rightful place in the cosmos, with every tear dried and every wound healed (Isa. 25:8; Jer. 30:17).

Needless to say, as with any serious illness, the diagnosis is not welcomed by the patient. Indeed, it is almost always vigorously denied and resisted. This is why the faithful Christian disciple is so often reviled and persecuted, and even put to death. For the direct and unveiled truth is precisely what human beings, caught up in the deceitful web of sin and evil, neither wish to know nor are able to bear. There is, moreover, a terrible irony which the faithful disciple encounters in every generation: that the church, the particular body to which Christ has entrusted this message of Good News, seems to develop a chronic immunity to the gospel even more resistant than that of the world. The result is that authentic discipleship often comes under sharpest attack from the Christian community itself. Those who claim the identity of Christian seem to be most stung by disciples who faithfully embody the ministry and teachings of Jesus of Nazareth.

Jesus warned that this would be so. He cautioned, firmly and candidly, about the cost of following him (Luke 14:25-30). To become his disciple was not to be undertaken lightly, but only after careful consideration (Luke 9:59-62). For the path of discipleship would mean sharing in the work he came to do, and which even now remains unfinished. Benefits there would be, but the commitment would be commensurably demanding. Rejection and persecution could not deter the faithful disciple, not even the cruelest kind of mistreatment, which would come from the church, or from family (Matt. 10:35-36).

Semantic Slippage

Once this sacrificial commitment becomes the ground rule for Christian discipleship, we cannot but observe that the word "discipleship" is employed very loosely today in the church, and nowhere more so than in the United States of America. On the one hand, it is used to describe the sacrificial life-style of those who have spurned the advantages of affluent living, and given themselves to serving the poor and the neglected. It is also applied to those who have paid the ultimate cost of discipleship, by surrendering their lives in obedience to Christ. Yet just as readily, *discipleship* is used to describe what happens week by week in thousands of local congregations across the United States, where millions of ordinary churchgoers do their best to live out the beliefs and practices of the Christian faith. Many of us are aware that our Christianity is highly conditioned by North American cultural values; yet even so, we endeavor to "make disciples," or "grow disciples," or persuade people to "take their discipleship seriously," or hope that they will "catch" the essence of true discipleship.

Not only is this discipleship rarely costly. All too often it is defined as a means of personal or social fulfillment, and presented as a package of benefits which, with minimal obligation, can be the acquisition of any who will align themselves with particular congregations. If further obligations are required at all, they are generally couched as *noblesse oblige*—the necessary duties of the advantaged. Such duties seldom call for more than minor generosities out of major resources, and usually carry the inducement of supplemental benefits. Rarely is it assumed that the normative requirements of Christian discipleship are the sacrifices and the disciplines of following the risen Jew of Nazareth.

These are of course sweeping statements to make, and it must immediately be conceded that there are many congregations in the United States where the responsibilities and disciplines of the Christian life are conscientiously practiced. By the same token, there are many pastoral leaders who are careful to rehearse the requirements of church membership with newcomers. Differing traditions will govern whether these come in the form of a critical invitation, or through catechesis and confirmation, or as new membership training. In the hands of a conscientious and competent pastor, however, they will always include the need for repentance, conversion, and faithful living in the power of the indwelling Holy Spirit.[1]

Christian Obligations

Yet in all traditions comprised by North American Christianity, we must ask how often prospective members are presented with the cost of their discipleship as they prepare for admission into the body of Christ. To what extent is sacrificial service stipulated as the *condition* of church membership? If a new convert is asked to engage in self-examination, is it not likely to be over the issues of forgiveness and reconciliation through Christ, and the spiritual experience of the new birth? If a catechumen is pressed in areas of accountability, is it not likely to be over particularities of doctrinal belief, and specifically those issues the pastor currently has on his or her agenda? And if obligations are reviewed with a prospective member, are they not likely to be those of programmatic commitment and institutional support?

In all candor we must further ask to what extent even these responsibilities are rehearsed with church members. For the flexible use of the word *discipleship* in the North American church has come to include the mildest interest in things religious, provided this interest draws toward church membership. What might be demanded of the new disciple in regard to worldly living is left to the exercise of personal choice or preference; which, in the cultural milieu of the late-twentieth-century United States, is tantamount to being cast adrift in a supermarket without price tags. Little wonder that so much congregational life is marked by the dereliction of basic Christian duties, and that so many potential disciples waver as they perceive their Christian commitment being subsumed by their churchly activities. Thinking church members can hardly be expected to wax enthusiastic over what can only be described as the planned obsolescence of their Christian identity.

President Jimmy Carter made an incisive comment on this gap in our church membership requirements in an address he gave at Emory University in 1987:

> I will have a group of men my age in a Sunday School class and see them sit around, fervent Christians, dedicated Christians enjoying the harmony and the fellowship of a community of various similar souls. Thanksgiving rolls around, and they say, Why don't we do something of a generous nature? Let us take up a collection and we will buy food, turkeys, etc. We will take this to some poor families and help them have a nice Thanksgiving. The next question is, who knows a poor family?

Generally the answer is, nobody in this class knows a poor family. Well, we will call the welfare office and get the name and address of a poor family. I think ministers ought to demand as a measure of character and achievement and status from their congregation, an active reaching out.[2]

There are, of course, many outreach ministries, sponsored by churches and movements of every theological persuasion, which reach boldly and charitably into the nation's social under-life. There are also whole denominations—The Salvation Army comes immediately to mind—who make such ministries their priority. But they tend to be the exception rather than the rule. For on any given Sunday morning, across the spectrum of North American churchly life, it would be difficult to infer from the great majority of congregations that those who gather in the name of Jesus Christ are truly representative of the Jew from Nazareth, whose closest companions were humble folk, and who was notorious for his association with the outcasts of his day.

Some years ago, in a midwestern mainline congregation, the youth of the church had an idea for a living parable. They decided to have one of their peers dress up as an indigent street person, and lie across the steps of the main entrance to the sanctuary on Sunday morning. Two more then placed themselves in a hidden vantage point with a video camera, and recorded what happened for the next thirty or forty minutes. As church members began to arrive, some drove up, saw the "tramp," and drove away, not even getting out of their car. Others parked, came up to the entrance, then looked for another way into the building. Others walked around him, over him, even peered down at him. But not one person made any effort to touch him, talk to him, help him, or even find out if he was alive.

The following Sunday, the youth group asked for permission to show the video to the congregation, and the discussion that followed, it was generally agreed, was one of the most significant times of repentance and critical commitment the members could recall.

Centripetal Ecclesial Inertia

The result of this prevailing self-centeredness in North American congregational life is what Robert Cushman has described as centripetal ecclesial inertia.[3] Energy there is aplenty; but almost all of it is expended on self-service. Overworked clergy find themselves bustling to meet the heightened expectations of members who have been encouraged to think of the church as a source of personal and communal enrichment, and are disappointed or disillusioned when these ideals do not materialize.[4] For clergy whose calling and theological training set their sights on far more weighty and hopeful issues of God's redemption, these demands are professionally and personally enervating. It is doubtful whether any group of people trained to this much knowledge and expertise are required to abandon their training so thoroughly and so quickly after assuming their professional responsibilities.

Laity are likewise frustrated, and to a much greater degree than they will express, by the fact that North American congregational life is so entangled in institutional self-maintenance. It comes as small comfort to learn that this is the pattern across the Christian world as a whole. David B. Barrett, whose monumental *World Christian Encyclopedia* (Oxford, 1982) is *sine qua non* for the serious student of Christianity, has collated some statistics which make sobering reading in this regard. As of 1988, Christians numbered some 33 percent of the world's population, but received an annual income of $8.6 trillion, or 62 percent of the world's total earnings. Of this, they spent 97 percent on themselves, donated 1 percent to secular charities, and spent only 2 percent on operating the structures of global Christianity. Of all Christians, 52 percent lived in affluence, 21 percent lived comfortably, 14 percent in near-poverty, and 13 percent (195 million) lived in absolute poverty. The annual income of organized Christianity was $160 billion, of which $152 billion (95 percent) was spent on home churches and their ministries. As just one example of this, the construction of new religious buildings in the United States burgeoned to $2.5 billion in 1987.[5]

All of this is not lost on the lay leadership of the North American church. Along with concerned Christians around the world, they are disturbed, not by the wealth of organized Christianity, but by how the wealth is spent. They are profoundly uneasy with congregational priorities, which seem to be designed chiefly to promote the benefits of Christian discipleship rather than their obligations to Jesus Christ in the world. They know only too well that religious consumerism has become entrenched, and that their Christian communities rarely function as channels of grace for the world. They also know that this is by no means an authentic Christian discipleship.

Pastoral Tensions

Before his untimely death in 1987, Orlando Costas, the brilliant Puerto Rican theologian, stated the dilemma with devastating insight. In *Christ Outside the Gate*, he described the Christian community in the United States of America as a clergy-dominated church with a laity-dominated clergy, propagating a gospel without demands, and demands without the gospel.[6] In this simple but telling observation, the problem is laid on clergy and laity alike. Laity find their discipleship stifled by patronizing or matronizing leadership from clergy, whose concern seems to be for the church far more than for the gospel. Clergy find their pastoral and prophetic ministries thwarted by laity who mistrust their credentials and refuse to be led.

The problem Costas so clearly identified stems from the fact that the agenda of congregations has been diverted from the calling and building up of Christian disciples. Instead of nurturing servants of Jesus Christ to be messengers of Good News for the world, churches seek to sustain the structures and programs which, properly used, facilitate this task, but which, in the absence of such purposeful engagement, are burdensome and demanding. The result is that clergy and laity alike have come to view Christian discipleship as a mindset rather than a life-style. Programs are developed, not to foster ministry and mission to the world, but to increase participation in churchly activities, and especially those activities centering on fellowship and the reinforcement of faithly perspectives.

This is not to suggest that vital congregational life is not integral to the Christian witness. We must be clear, however, that this is not the meaning and purpose of Christian discipleship, but is merely among its benefits, to be placed alongside weighty obligations. When we examine the scriptural invitation to discipleship, we find that Jesus was blunt, if not brutal: "If any one comes to me and does not hate his own father and mother and wife and children and brothers and sisters, yes, and even his own life, he cannot be my disciple. Whoever does not bear his own cross and come after me, cannot be my disciple" (Luke 14:26-27). If this is not what we present to prospective church members as the condition of their discipleship; if this is not what we demand of our existing members; if instead we produce programs and strategies and models, all designed to induce their continuing participation in our congregational life to their greatest advantage; then either the word *disciple* has come to mean something very different from what Jesus meant by it, or those of us in the North American church who

continue to invite people to become Christian disciples on these terms
are irresponsible, or worse, dishonest.

Sacrificial Challenges

Our semantic slippage is further compounded by many of our
paradigms for faithful discipleship, which reflect the very sacrificial
life-style we fail to demand of one another in our congregational life
and work. Take, for example, the recent pictorial biography, *Dietrich
Bonhoeffer: A Life in Pictures.*[7] Tracing his family ancestry back to the
sixteenth century, it lays out an impressive pedigree of civil leadership
and service, and highly respectable contributions to German academic
life. The dignity with which his family bore the cost of his faithfulness
to the Christ who is Jesus of Nazareth, as opposed to the Jesus who so
often is the cultic Christ, is therefore deeply poignant, as in the
following extract from a letter written to a colleague in Boston by his
father, Karl Bonhoeffer. It is dated October 8, 1945, after the fall of the
Nazi regime, and when the fullness of the cost to the family had finally
become clear:

> I understand that you have heard that we have had a bad time and lost
> two sons (Dietrich the theologian and Klaus the head of Lufthansa) and
> two sons-in-law (Professors Schleicher and Dohnanyi) at the hands of
> the Gestapo. You can imagine that that has not been without its effect on
> us old folks. For years we had the tension caused by anxiety for those
> arrested and for those not yet arrested but in danger. But since we were
> all agreed on the need to act . . . and [my sons] had resolved if necessary
> to lay down their lives, we are sad but also proud of their attitude, which
> has been consistent.[8]

This biography is disturbing because it places the events of those
years in proper perspective. For much of what Bonhoeffer and others
discerned, and finally resisted at the cost of their lives, was perceived
by others to be nothing out of the ordinary. On the contrary, it was a
time of revived pride for Germans, a re-affirmation of their national
identity, drawing on a deep-rooted mythology from their past. Today,
with hindsight, and with the recognition given to Christian martyrs,
we applaud their costly discipleship. We even use Bonhoeffer's
devotional writings for our spiritual formation, and study his ethics in
our classrooms. But at the time, in the manipulative propaganda of a

spreading Nazi domination, it was not at all easy to discern what was happening. How did one respond when the ecclesial hierarchy, bent on survival rather than faithfulness to the gospel, censured those who tried to hold fast to the central, scriptural, ethical truths of the gospel? How to respond when Reich Bishop Müller "nationalized" the Sermon on the Mount, changing "Blessed are the meek" to "Blessed is the one who is a good comrade at all times. He will get on well in the world"?[9]

As we know, the confessing church of Germany was not silent. There was the Barmen Declaration of 1934, and there were many who took their stand, humbly and anonymously. As Bonhoeffer himself wrote in 1942:

> Are we still of any use?
> We have been silent witnesses of evil deeds: we have been drenched by many storms; we have learnt the arts of equivocation and pretence; experience has made us suspicious of others and kept us from being truthful and open; intolerable conflicts have worn us down and even made us cynical. Are we still of any use?
> What we shall need is not geniuses, or cynics, or misanthropes, or clever tactitioners, but plain, honest, straightforward men. Will our inward power of resistance be strong enough, and our honesty with ourselves remorseless enough, for us to find our way back to simplicity and straightforwardness?[10]

The directness of such questions of discipleship is captured by the photograph on the front cover of the book. It is a normal scene, so normal as to be chilling. The year is 1931, when things are already headed toward their cataclysmic outcome. Bonhoeffer is standing at the door of his church after morning worship, talking to a friend, as many of us so often do. People are passing in the street, headed for their Sunday lunch. It is all so very churchly; but also so very deceptive. For it was in the midst of such ecclesial enculturation that Bonhoeffer, and others like him, had to take a stand. And what stays with us in his devotional writings, especially those from his closing months in prison, is his personal obedience; a discipleship that was radical and therefore costly.

Not that Bonhoeffer is our only modern paradigm. In her book *Six Modern Martyrs,* Mary Craig selects five others to join him: Martin Luther King, Jr., civil rights leader and prophet; Father Maximilian Kolbe, a Polish Franciscan who laid down his life for a married fellow prisoner in Auschwitz; Janani Luwum, the Anglican Archbishop of Uganda, murdered by Idi Amin in 1977; Oscar Romero, the Catholic

Archbishop of San Salvador, gunned down in 1977 in the very act of the eucharist; and Sister Maria Skobstsova, a Russian Orthodox nun who helped the Jews in German-occupied France, and perished at Ravensbruck.[11] There are of course many more we could list; but countless more we cannot, quite simply because they are nameless. Some of them carry the title of Christian martyr; many do not, because they were not Christian. But their places of honor at the heavenly banquet are already reserved. And on that day, with complete hindsight, we shall begrudge them their elevated status not one whit.

Then there are the less dramatic stories of our Christian contemporaries around the world, whose faithful discipleship is nonetheless in marked contrast to our own. There are pastors in Fiji, for example, who have charge of many congregations, with thousands of members scattered over a wide area. They must make their rounds on foot, not having the resources for mechanized transport, as they minister to their people and supervise the lay *catechists* who serve as local congregational leaders. Such pastors have one objective only: to help their people become better Christian disciples. Anything else would be a waste of their time.

There are the Protestant lay pastors in Latin America, many of whom work at secular occupations so that congregations unable to support them full-time might still have a ministry. Even if they were full-time, they would receive a minimal stipend, well below $100 a month. One such pastor from Guatemala recently visited United Methodist congregations in the United States to talk about his discipleship. He spoke of the twenty-seven widows in one of his congregations, whose husbands had all been killed during the past year by right-wing death squads. The eloquence of his testimony lay in his prosaic description of what it means to be faithful to the demands of following Jesus Christ, as opposed to merely praising his name. Each morning, he told us, is a deep experience of grace, an opportunity to thank God that it is the light of daybreak which has awakened him, and not the dreaded knock on the door at 3:00 A.M. As one of his hosts remarked, that puts our North American 50-minute pastoral counseling sessions in an altogether different perspective.

Consumerist Contrasts

Indeed, our pastoral concerns as a whole in the United States could hardly be more in contrast. Although there are instances where North

American pastors are serving in circumstances of moderate or even severe hardship, it would be difficult to find any denomination, or any part of the country, in which a substantial number of clergy are living below the poverty line, as they do in so many Third World countries. Housing, medical and insurance benefits, and a minimum salary are regarded as normative working conditions in the United States, without which a prospective pastor will probably look elsewhere for employment. To accept penury in order to fulfill pastoral obligations is rarely a serious option. And though there are those who make courageous stands on issues of prophetic ministry, and many others who suffer the subtle harassments of criticism, ridicule, and even vilification, again it would be difficult to find instances where this has exacted a toll on anything like the scale we find in Latin America today.

From a lay perspective, it would be no less difficult to find instances in North America where the cost of joining a Christian community is torture and loss of life. On the contrary, as we have noted, the measure of congregational life is the efficacy of programs and activities in meeting personal and interpersonal needs. People will "shop" for the church of their choice, and seek those forms of "discipleship" which are self-evidently fulfilling. So thoroughly does this consumerism govern our churchly life that we have come to shape our congregational priorities far more by popular response than by the imperatives of the gospel. This critique of consumerism does not suggest that the wishes and needs of people should be intentionally neglected in setting pastoral goals and objectives. But when the costly discipleship of Christian colleagues elsewhere in the world presses us with basic questions about the nature and purpose of our own discipleship, it is altogether inappropriate to justify our ecclesial centripetal inertia on the grounds of popular demand.

In matters of Christian discipleship, this needs-based demand is precisely what cannot and must not be allowed to govern our priorities. For whenever the efficacy of pastoral ministry is judged by public response, the first casualty is the mission of church, which is to say God's mission of healing and salvation for planet Earth. There are times when the Christian disciple will be welcomed as the bearer of Good News and an agent of God's grace. But there are times when the truth of the gospel, with its simplicity and candor, will offend. The disciple must therefore learn to weather stiff if not violent resistance, and ignore those who would counsel a less confrontative approach. On this, as on everything else, Jesus was clear and candid about what his followers could expect:

Do not think that I have come to bring peace on earth; I have not come to bring peace, but a sword. For I have come to set a man against his father, and a daughter against her mother, and a daughter-in-law against her mother-in-law; and a man's foes will be those of his own household. (Matt. 10:34-36)

As they were going along the road, a man said to him, "I will follow you wherever you go." And Jesus said to him, "Foxes have holes, and birds of the air have nests; but the Son of man has nowhere to lay his head." (Luke 9:57-58)

And Jesus was never more serious than when he repudiated Peter's rejection of his impending passion and death (Matt. 16:23; Mark 8:33).

Solutions and Pitfalls

Although there are many persons in the church today, both clergy and lay, who are deeply disturbed by this state of affairs, when it comes to solutions there is little general agreement. Too many pitfalls await each proposal. Some leaders advocate spiritual renewal, rightly pointing out that the Christian life must be grounded in a vital, growing relationship with the risen Christ in the power of the Holy Spirit. This, they further point out, opens the church to spiritual gifts, identified so clearly in the early church, and here for us today if only we will avail ourselves of them: gifts of prophecy, service, teaching, wisdom, healing, tongues, interpretation, intercession, and others.[12]

The pitfall of this solution is that spiritual gifts can easily become the goal of discipleship rather than the unexpected and unmerited blessing of living and working with Jesus Christ in the world. Jesus himself was very clear about this with his first disciples: Though the blessings of following him would be rich, these blessings could not be their motive in making their decision. And the difficulty with much of the spiritual renewal promoted in the United States is precisely this inversion of priorities. So important does religious experience become, that it is viewed by many as the true mark of authentic discipleship, and therefore to be pursued ahead of all other objectives, if need be by taking shortcuts.

Spiritual Amphetamines

These shortcuts can best be described as spiritual amphetamines, and their consumption has reached epidemic proportions. The problem has worsened because, like any amphetamine, they work. They appear to recapture and revitalize spirituality in the disciple for the very good reason that this is exactly what happens—for a time. It is when the task of discipleship requires sustained, dedicated, laborious work, however, without reward and with no evident results, that a striving for heightened spirituality is exposed for what it is: a misuse of the true gifts of the Holy Spirit. The purpose of spiritual gifts is not personal fulfillment, but succor and hope for others. These gifts are not for consumption, but for sharing with the rest of the world.

The more unsavory of these amphetamines need not occupy us here. But one that is widely used in North American churches does require a cautionary word: the proliferation of small groups. They are found everywhere in the life and work of the church, and in some instances have become the basis for entire congregational structures—though it is interesting to note that the church began to take small groups seriously at about the time sociologists had come to regard them as somewhat outmoded.[13] This is not to imply that small groups *per se* are undesirable. On the contrary, they are a given of human society. Moreover, the wealth of sociological and anthropological studies now available on the subject allows us to understand much more fully how best they can be used in the mission and ministry of the church. The pitfall, however, is that instead of using them to further spiritual growth or to develop Christian discipleship, pastors and congregations tend to use them as a substitute for these properly Christian objectives.

Therein lies their danger as an amphetamine. North American culture is so highly individualistic that people are starved of genuine human relationships; and once they encounter the interpersonal cohesiveness of a small group, they are overwhelmed by what they are missing in their day-to-day lives. Whatever the occasion of the small group, therefore, be it prayer, Bible study, personal sharing, marriage enrichment, and so on, the experience of vital interaction with other human beings, rather than the purpose for which the group was formed, can easily become the measure of what takes place. And where this dynamic is not adequately understood, it becomes an amphetamine, exhausting spiritual energies in pursuit of interpersonal experiences having little bearing on the realities of daily Christian living.

Even more dangerous is the propensity of this amphetamine to foster gnosticism, which always seems latent in Christian experience. It is beyond the scope of our study to delve into what is a very complicated subject, going all the way back to New Testament Christianity. But if we can define gnosticism very generally as the concept of privileged access to God through secret knowledge, we have a sense of its potential for mischief in much of our contemporary spiritual renewal, and especially in its small group expressions.

This has recently been well expounded by Philip Lee in his fascinating volume, *Against the Protestant Gnostics*. Although his arguments are open to discussion, his conclusions are highly pertinent to our present North American dilemma, in that he recommends a return to the central teachings of the Judeo-Christian tradition, and especially to those of the Old Testament, which gnosticism tends to devalue, in order to focus again on the task of discipleship.[14] And in this regard, small groups can serve a significant twofold function: mutual accountability for the task in hand with trusted Christian colleagues, and discernment of the presence and power of the Holy Spirit through candid Christian sharing.

Worldly Involvements

Another solution to the dilemma of North American discipleship is the advocacy of a deeper commitment to social justice. By taking the incarnational ministry of Jesus as the touchstone, those who advocate this form of discipleship seek to involve themselves and the church in work that prepares for the coming reign of God. If a paradigmatic chapter from the New Testament could be cited for this, it would be Matthew 25, with the parables of the wise and foolish bridesmaids, the talents, and the sheep and the goats.

In one of the most significant books to appear on evangelism in recent years, *Five Lanterns at Sundown*, Alfred C. Krass takes the first of these parables as an allegory of the church as messenger to the world.[15] Rather than an invitation to be saved, the message of the church is an announcement: Be Ready! As we observed at the beginning of this chapter, that is precisely what makes the authentic Christian disciple such an awkward person for the world to hear and heed. It is difficult enough for people to be told that they are sick and need to be healed. But when they are further told that the physician is proceeding with the cure, with or without their permission, the message is truly disturbing. In effect, it presents them with an ultimatum. Instead of the gospel being a personal invitation to salvation, a choice they can consider to their advantage, it becomes a historical and eternal reality in which their lack of participation will not only cost them very dearly but also will ultimately be quite pointless. For the reign of God is coming, whether or not they are ready.

Since Christian disciples are commissioned to make this announcement to the world, then clearly they must show the way. Krass reinforces this point by citing Karl Donfried's exegesis of the oil in the lamps of the wise bridesmaids as the good works we do while we wait for the arrival of the groom.[16] And since good works cannot be shared, but only performed or neglected, the foolish bridesmaids are left out in the cold (Matt. 25:10-13). The other two parables make even more clear that active expectancy is the appropriate attitude for faithful disciples. The number of talents given to each of the servants is less important than what they did with what they had been given (Matt. 25:29). And in evaluating the sheep and the goats, it is not their belief in Christ which gains the nations of the world a favorable judgment at the end of history, but what they have done for him. Common to both the sheep and the goats are the recognition of Jesus for who he is, and their surprise at how they are being evaluated. Those who have fed the hungry, clothed the naked, and visited the hospitals and the jails, have been doing the work of Christ, irrespective of their personal beliefs. Whereas those who have neglected these basic works of mercy have been offending Christ, again irrespective of their beliefs (Matt. 25:45).

There are many faithful Christians today in the United States who take these parables very much to heart. They refuse to be sidetracked into what they perceive to be an unduly spiritualized faith, and a discipleship "too heavenly minded to be of any earthly use." They are wearied by those who profess faith in a Christ who bears little if any resemblance to Jesus of Nazareth, and by those whose concerns for a deeper faith seem to focus on spiritual birth and infancy to the detriment of spiritual growth and maturity. They find the common sense of the epistle of James far more pertinent to the priorities of discipleship in the world: If someone is shivering, give her a coat, and only then comfort her with words; if someone is hungry, the question of spiritual food is altogether moot until his stomach has been filled (James 2:15-17).

It is this dynamic which prompts so many of the social ministries of churches throughout the country, to say nothing of those congregations and religious orders which make it their business to be about the work of feeding the hungry, clothing the naked, and visiting the sick and imprisoned. And it is this same dynamic which impels persons, groups, and congregations to be involved in the larger issues of justice and peace. By disciples such as these, the secular powers of the world are reminded that the God whom Jesus described as loving and parental is also the God whose law was delivered from Sinai, and who will exact a strict account from those to whom much power has been temporarily delegated for the benefit of all.

Utopian Tendencies

It is not surprising that this approach to discipleship should draw much of its inspiration from the Old Testament; and rightly so, for the Hebrew bible is an integral part of the Christian scriptures, and Jesus made clear that he regarded himself as fulfilling the law and the prophets. Yet herein lies the pitfall of this solution to our discipleship dilemma—the tendency to overlook the personal relationship with Christ which is the necessary bedrock and wellspring of faithful Christian living. It is not obedience to God's laws of justice, peace, and love that marks the authentic disciple, but obedience to the Christ who embodies that law. It is not the utopian vision of the world that motivates and empowers the disciple, but the indwelling Holy Spirit, the Spirit of Christ. Without such an intimate, spiritual relationship, concerned disciples can easily become zealots, driven by ideals neither they nor anyone else is able to fulfill.

This pitfall is an important reason why radical discipleship so often becomes alienated from the churches fostering it, as frustration with ambivalent support or lack of understanding presses faithful disciples to seek collegiality elsewhere. In so doing, there is often a subtle surrender of identity, which weakens their particular source of strength. This is not to suggest that Christians have proprietary rights on preparing for God's *shalom*, still less a monopoly on God's grace. But it is to contend that Christian disciples must be clear about their particular role in the panorama of God's saving work in the world. They are a special task force, accountable to Christ for all things at all times. That many who claim this identity seem to have lost their way is no good reason to seek alternative alignments. For in so doing, there is the grave risk of losing one's Christian identity altogether.

Contextual Realities

Neither of these solutions, however—a heightened spirituality nor a greater commitment to social justice—resolves the dilemma of our North American discipleship. Ultimately, both approaches refuse to accept the broad range of commitment an enculturated congregation inevitably entails. Those who advocate a deeper commitment of faith are confronted week by week with large numbers of church members who seem to be indifferent or even immune to spiritual exhortation. It is not that all these members are spiritually bereft; they would not be at church at all if they were. They are simply not ready for the intensity of faith that seems to be the criterion for this form of discipleship.

By the same token, those who advocate greater commitment to social justice encounter caution and even fear on the part of many church members who do not wish to be involved in activities that press their personal faith to more public expressions and embodiments. Again, it is not that these members are insensitive to poverty and oppression. But even those who are regular and faithful in attending to the needs of the poor are not always ready for the political implications of working for the coming reign of God.

Accordingly, the rank-and-file church member is often labeled a "nominal Christian" by the advocates of spiritual renewal and social justice alike. And though the phrase usually means something quite different in their respective connotations, at times of deep discouragement (and there are many) it means exactly the same: that the majority of church members are not taking their discipleship seriously, and do not merit the identity of Christian. They are not the real thing. They are an illusion. They are not the church.

But the fact of the matter is that they *are* the church. They are there in attendance, week by week. Without their financial contributions, many of the outreach ministries and much of the work of the church in social justice would not be possible. Nor would the advocates of spiritual renewal wish to suggest that Sunday morning congregations be restricted to those who meet their spiritual criteria. Whoever they are, whatever their depth of commitment, they are welcome.

The Crux of the Dilemma

It should now be clear why the focus of this study has to be the United States of America. This is where the dilemma of discipleship is most acute, because this is where the church is most integral to its cultural environment. To borrow somewhat tenuously from Paul's vision, if the whole creation is waiting for the children of God to be

revealed (Rom. 8:19), then the rest of the world church is waiting for
the North American church to assume its proper role in global
Christianity. This is not by way of money and political clout, though
that is unfortunately how it is most often perceived and practiced. It is
rather by way of what a church can and ought to be in a country where
the Christian witness has been given a very prolonged and extensive
opportunity to make an impact. That our present attitudes tend to
focus primarily on our own ecclesial concerns taxes the Christian
collegiality and increasingly evokes the impatience and irritation of our
sisters and brothers around the world.

Not to beat about the bush, the United States of America is the most
churched country in the world. Yes, there are signs of phenomenal
growth among younger churches elsewhere in the world, and an
awesome working of God's grace in places of oppression and injustice.
But the fact remains that the United States is a country where
Christians have been given an opportunity to influence a culture with
the gospel message to an extent quite unprecedented in the history of
the church.

In 1985, George Gallup, Jr., published a composite survey, culled
from the past fifty years of that organization's work. During this
half-century, membership in churches and synagogues in the United
States has ranged between 67 percent and 76 percent of the
population, and most recently stands at 68 percent. In a typical week in
1984, four out of ten adults attended church. In 1985, 87 percent of the
population prayed at least occasionally, and 31 percent prayed twice or
more each day. From 1944 to 1981, between 94 percent and 97 percent
of Americans said they believed in God, the most recent figure being 95
percent. And, perhaps most strikingly, some three quarters of the
population have consistently affirmed their belief in the divinity of
Christ, the most recent figure being 70 percent.[17]

It might be argued that, significant though they are, these statistics
are not unprecedented; that they are well surpassed by centuries of
Christendom. So we need to be clear that the precedent of this
particular churched culture and enculturated church is that all of this
has happened in a sociopolitical setting which has, for at least two
hundred years, intentionally resisted the structural criteria of
Christendom. Moreover, as the North American church has pro-
gressed through its history, it has come to reflect its cultural
environment, and become predominantly voluntaristic. It is this which
gives it a special place in world Christianity, whether or not it fulfills
its role.

Two Crucial Questions

The dilemma comes down, therefore, to two crucial questions. Is this large, enculturated church a valid expression of the body of Christ, just as it is, with all of its indifference, ambivalence, and centripetal inertia? And is there validity in describing the members of such a church as Christian disciples, given the contrast between the folk Christianity of the many, and the costly discipleship of the few? The answers to these questions profoundly govern how we understand the gospel of Jesus Christ, how we proclaim it, and how we live it out—in short, how we function as the church in the world.

It is the same dilemma that has faced the church across the centuries; and with the spread of global Christianity, it will face more and more churches in our own day and age. Will dedicated, committed disciples invariably find themselves isolated in their endeavor to live out their commitment to Christ? Are they fated to tread a lonely path in the typical North American congregation, hoping that colleagues will one day join them, but not really expecting it to happen? Is the average congregation of an established church destined always to be hopelessly enculturated, playing an important sacralizing role in the community but never really shining as the beacon of God's saving grace for the world?

Or is there an understanding of discipleship and congregational life alike that can provide a clear, complementary identity, so that together they might form the sign community Jesus intended the church to be? To answer this question, we must enquire more closely into the meaning of Christian discipleship, and the nature of God's salvation.

PARTICULAR VOCATION: CHRISTIAN DISCIPLESHIP

Early Origins

Having argued that an unduly flexible use of *discipleship* in the church of today is presenting us with a serious dilemma, and most especially in the enculturated church of North America, our first step toward clarification must be to examine the word's origins in the Christian tradition. For this, we must of course go back to the ministry of Jesus himself. But before we do, it will be helpful to have a more general sense of the word. For one thing, Jesus is by no means the only great religious leader to have had disciples; nor, for that matter, is he the only rabbi in the New Testament whose followers are so identified. The Pharisees had disciples (Mark 2:18); and so did his cousin John the Baptist, as Jesus acknowledged when he sent word of his credentials with them to John in prison (Matt. 11:2-4).

The English word *disciple* comes most directly from the Latin, *discipulus*, meaning "a pupil." This is not in the sense that we have come to use it today when speaking of public education, nor yet in the sense of the Hellenistic-Roman *gymnasium*, where learning was largely a matter of memorizing a basic core curriculum.[1] Derived from the verb *discere*, meaning "to learn," it was used in the Roman world more in the sense of someone who takes lessons from a coach. Without necessarily implying a close relationship, the connotation was that of learning from a particular teacher, the privileged form of education for those who could afford it.

Our Christian understanding of the word, however, has come to us primarily through its usage in the New Testament, where we find it with two applications. In general, as we have noted, it is applied to the followers of religious leaders, and by association to those who affirm their teachings—as in Jesus' dispute with the Pharisees over his authority in restoring sight to a blind man on the sabbath (John 9:27f.). Even when it pertains to Jesus' own disciples, it has a much broader application than the twelve with whom it is most often identified. Jesus himself uses it to describe what appears to be a very wide following (John 8:30-31), and other references indicate that there were many others besides the small inner circle (Matt. 8:21-23; Luke 6:13, 19:37; John 11:54).

The particular use of the word, on the other hand, is the one with which we are most familiar, namely, to identify the twelve whom Jesus called to follow him, and who are named (Matt. 10:1-4). The distinction between these and the larger following is most clearly drawn in John's Gospel, after Jesus has identified himself as the "bread of life." There we read that "many of his disciples drew back and no longer went about with him." When Jesus asks the twelve whether they too are going to leave him, Simon Peter answers with the words that have come to be for many the truest mark of discipleship: "Lord, to whom shall we go? You have the words of eternal life; and we have believed, and have come to know, that you are the Holy One of God" (John 6:66-69).

Close Relationship

When we examine the relationship Jesus had with these twelve, we find the concept of discipleship developed in some depth. The best analogy here would be the role of the graduate student in academic life, or the apprentice in a craft or profession. Implied in this is a closeness of relationship, a directness of interaction, which is at once more intimate and more influential on the student than that of a large classroom, or even a personal tutor. In choosing a professor, a graduate student expresses not only keen interest in a field of study, but also a willingness to explore that field under the guidance of a particular mentor. In this way, the student learns from the insights of a leading mind. By sharing the knowledge that impels to further research, teacher and student together share the excitement of mutual discovery. In learning a craft or a profession, the apprentice works alongside the one who is skilled. By assisting, practicing, observing, and emulating, the apprentice acquires the expertise and the experience necessary to join that craft or profession.

These analogies, however, must be qualified in one important respect. The graduate student will one day emerge as a scholar in his or her own right, and in some instances will exceed the accomplishments of the teacher. The apprentice will one day become a peer member of a craft or profession in his or her own right, and may even excel the teacher. But when it comes to being a Christian disciple, Jesus makes very clear that the relationship will always be that of follower:

> A disciple is not above his teacher, nor a servant above his master; it is enough for the disciple to be like his teacher, and the servant like his master. (Matt. 10:24-25)[2]

This will have profound implications when we come to explore the nature of discipleship in the church of today, and especially the discernment of leadership in congregational life and work.

The Twelve

But first, what does the New Testament tell us about the relationship between Jesus and the twelve? The book in which this model of discipleship is most developed is the Gospel according to Matthew. Here we find more references to the twelve than in any other Gospel, and in fact the only references to their being twelve in number.[3] It is also the only Gospel in which we find the word *ekklēsia*, signifying the gathering of early Christian disciples into the church (Matt. 16:18, 18:17). In a significant new study, *House of Disciples*, Michael H. Crosby points out the connection between the Greek word for disciple, *mathētēs* (one who has been taught), and *Matthaios*, the author of this Gospel.[4] Whether he was the Matthew of the twelve, or a Jewish Christian, or a Gentile knowledgeable in the Hebrew tradition and scripture, matters less than the fact that he was writing for a New Testament community. By its very name, therefore, this is a book about discipleship. It is a detailed record not only of how Jesus taught his disciples, but also of how the early church saw its task in living out that teaching in the world. This first Gospel "continually links true discipleship with being taught, understanding what has been taught, and putting it into practice."[5]

Authority

Matthew makes clear at the outset that the basis of discipleship is the call of Jesus, made with the authority *(exousia)* given to him by God through the Holy Spirit. When we read that Simon, Andrew, James, and John leave their nets and follow him, we are given no other reason than that Jesus called them and gave them a new task. His invitation carried the authority of a command (Matt. 4:18-22).[6] It is the same authority Jesus gives to the disciples when he sends them out to proclaim the imminence of the kingdom of heaven (Matt. 10:1, 5-7; Mark 6:7; Luke 9:1). It gives them power over disease and infirmity, and assurance in confrontation with the authorities of this world (Matt. 10:18-20).

In this warning to his disciples that they can expect to be persecuted, Jesus says much about the extent of his authority, and theirs. They are bound to come into conflict with the world, because their authority will confront spiritual wickedness in high places. Since evil reigns in the world—in persons, societies, institutions, and centers of worldly authority—to that extent Jesus' power and authority will inevitably counter the demonic. God's *exousia* will prevail, but the demonic powers will not give up without a struggle.

Thus the Pharisees are quick to attribute Jesus' authority to that of Beelzebul, the prince of demons. They rightly perceive the field of conflict, even as they misjudge the battle lines (Matt. 12:24; John 8:52, 10:20). In his reply, Jesus tries to show them where they are mistaken. It is not only that his power comes from God. His healing and his exorcism of the demonic are also inextricably linked with his proclamation of the kingdom of God, the coming *shalom* of the Messiah. The demons he casts out of persons are the same demonic forces that pervert worldly authority with injustice and oppression. That he should be about such business in the name of Beelzebul, therefore, is patently nonsensical (Matt. 12:22-32). His disciples, in their exercise of his power, will likewise encounter demonic opposition at every point of confrontation, be it pain, disease, oppression, injustice, tyranny—in short, anything standing in the way of the coming reign of God.[7]

Jesus' authority is also directly linked with the spiritual authority given to the prophets who preceded him. Since he has given this same authority to his disciples, they join him in that lineage of prophetic ministry to the world:

He who receives you receives me, and he who receives me receives him who sent me. He who receives a prophet because he is a prophet shall receive a prophet's reward, and he who receives a righteous man because he is a righteous man shall receive a righteous man's reward. And whoever gives to one of these little ones even a cup of cold water because he is a disciple, truly, I say to you, he shall not lose his reward. (Matt. 10:40-42)[8]

Jesus goes even farther. He identifies his disciples as a new, inaugural family of God:

While he was still speaking to the people, behold, his mother and his brothers stood outside, asking to speak to him. But he replied to the man who told him, "Who is my mother, and who are my brothers?" And stretching out his hand toward his disciples, he said, "Here are my mother and my brothers! For whoever does the will of my Father in heaven is my brother, and sister, and mother." (Matt 12:46-50; cf. Mark 3:31-35; Luke 8:19-21)

To Fulfill All Righteousness

The key to this relationship, however, is not just knowing the will of God. It is also doing it. For if the basis of discipleship in Matthew is the call of Jesus, the essence is understanding his teaching and putting it into practice.[9] The word which best expresses this is *dikaiosunē*, most often translated in the New Testament as "righteousness." When Jesus asks John to baptize him, it is "to fulfil all righteousness" (Matt. 3:15). In the Sermon on the Mount, he proclaims that "blessed are those who hunger and thirst for righteousness," and blessed are those who are "persecuted for righteousness' sake, for theirs is the kingdom of heaven" (Matt. 5:6, 10). Whoever "relaxes one of the least of" the commandments of the law shall be called "least in the kingdom of heaven," but those who practice and teach these commandments shall be called "great in the kingdom of heaven. For I tell you, unless your righteousness exceeds that of the scribes and Pharisees, you will never enter the kingdom of heaven" (Matt. 5:19-20).

Unfortunately, through various contextual traditionings and translations, this word, so pivotal to understanding the nature and purpose of Christian discipleship, has lost much of its original meaning. It has acquired legalistic overtones it was never meant to convey, primarily because it has come to be dissociated from its relational origins as a theocentric concept. *Righteousness* will inevitably be misunderstood and misapplied when it is not viewed as overwhelmingly God-centered. Any righteousness human beings might evince will never be anything other than a gracious gift from God.

The Righteousness of God

The idea of righteousness as an inner quality of God was given its most eloquent scriptural expression by the eighth-century prophets of the Old Testament. In *The Distinctive Ideas of the Old Testament*, Norman H. Snaith points out that these prophets not only gave a new content to the idea of *holiness* by linking it with the idea of *righteousness*, but also did so in a way altogether different from the moral ideas of the Greeks. The concept required further development, of course, notably in Jeremiah and Second-Isaiah. But with the divine attribute of *ṣedeq* and *ṣedaqah* (the masculine and feminine forms of the word) there emerged the distinctive notion that humankind sees the holiness of God, not only in worship of the wholly Other, but also by the exaltation of righteousness in their midst.[10]

The original meaning of *ṣedeq* was "to be straight," a divine standard by which people and things could be measured. However, the eighth-century prophets gave it what Snaith describes as "a deep-seated and fundamental bias . . . for the poor and down-trodden."[11] This did not mean that the poor and oppressed were to receive better things than everyone else, nor yet that "wrong actions which are condemned in the rich are to be condoned in the poor."[12] But it did mean that, with no one else to help them, the helpless could count on God; and that as long as humanity tended to neglect such persons, God's righteousness would insist on putting things right.

It cannot be emphasized too strongly that this concept of righteousness is not an abstract ideal, but a pronouncement of the nature and the will of God. Thus the indignation of Amos is at the incongruity between the elaborate worship rituals of his day, and the glaring injustices of the rich (Amos 5:22f.). Likewise, Hosea's charges against covenant-breaking Israel detail the widespread lawlessness which follows from such breaches of faith. Steadfast love and knowledge of God are preferable by far to sacrifice and burnt offerings (Hos. 6:6-10).

And from Micah, we have perhaps the best-known declaration of all:

> With what shall I come before the Lord,
>   and bow myself before God on high?
> Shall I come before him with burnt offerings,
>   with calves a year old? . . .
> He has showed you, O man, what is good;
>   and what does the Lord require of you
> but to do justice, and to love kindness,
>   and to walk humbly with your God?
>
> (Mic. 6:6, 8)

The Justice of God

Snaith further points out that the Hebrew word for justice, *mišpat*, is closely associated with *sedeq-sedaqah*, and is just as theocentric in its meaning. Since the Hebrew concept of God, unlike that of the Hellenistic world, is that of a deity involved in the day-to-day affairs of the world, the word *mišpat* is not an ethereal quality, remotely divine, but the concrete and intrusive declarations of a God with an agenda—and a very biased agenda at that. For those who would practice this *mišpat* as Micah advocates, it means nothing less than "doing God's will as it has been made clear in past experience."[13]

It is in Second-Isaiah, however, that the concept of God's righteousness comes to its fullest meaning. In the eighth-century prophets, *sedeq-sedaqah* had been used in an ethical sense, albeit with God's active and biased participation in the world on behalf of the poor and the helpless. But in Second-Isaiah it is developed into a concept of salvation in which God's righteousness is not only pronounced, but where it ultimately triumphs and prospers. "Israel is saved by the Lord / with everlasting salvation" (Isa. 45:17), and the holiness of God is brought "into the center of the salvation vocabulary."[14]

In other words, the righteousness of God is not only an ethical standard, not only a proactive participation in applying that standard, not only a participation weighted in favor of those who cannot help themselves, but also an ultimate vindication of that standard in its universal triumph and victory. God is not only a righteous and a saving God. God is righteous *because* God saves. "There is no other god besides me, / a righteous God and a Savior; / there is none besides me" (Isa. 45:21).

This theocentric concept of justice-righteousness becomes even more specific for the Christian, because the God whose will the

Christian seeks to understand and practice is the God who is revealed in Jesus Christ. The difficulty in interpreting the New Testament directives in this regard lies in the fact that the Greek word, *dikaiosunē*, whether translated "righteousness" (Matt. 5:6), or "justice" (Acts 24:25) or "justification" (Gal. 2:21), or piety (Matt. 6:1), or "all that is right" (Eph. 5:9), tends to be caught up in the ethical or philosophical abstractions of its Hellenistic context. Only when the full weight of its Old Testament prophetic connotation is brought to bear—a connotation which, as we have noted, Jesus made altogether explicit in the synagogue at Nazareth—do we have the understanding of discipleship which the Gospel of Matthew unfolds for us. God's will, which is to say God's justice, which is to say God's righteousness, which is to say God's bias toward the poor and the helpless, which is to say God's universal salvation, is precisely the knowledge of God the disciple of Jesus of Nazareth must seek out; and having sought it out, the disciple must put it into practice in every possible dimension of his or her daily life.

Entering the Reign of God

Thus the need for the new family alignments which Jesus identified for his disciples. Not only would they have to be willing to sever former family ties and make new ones (Matt. 12:46-50). They would also find themselves rejected and even victimized by their own blood relatives (Matt 10:21). To be a disciple of Jesus meant nothing less than entering a whole new realm, the fullness of eternal life, the coming reign of God (Matt. 6:33; Mark 10:29f.; Luke 18:29f.). And for this, one had to seek after righteousness: hunger and thirst for it, and suffer for it (Matt. 5:6, 10).

The particularity of this righteousness was made clear when Jesus was approached by the rich young ruler (Matt. 19:16-22). Even when Jesus had indicated that the way to eternal life was to keep God's commandments, the young man still pressed him. His quest was still elusive. What more did he have to do? Jesus' answer was very specific, yet very open. The righteousness of God for which the young man yearned did not consist of isolated deeds, but of a whole reordering of his life: a realignment of his wealth, his possessions, and his status. And this, as we know, he was unwilling to do.

In the Gospel according to Luke, the same question drew from Jesus one of the best-known stories of all time, the good Samaritan

(10:25-37). This anonymous agent of mercy has become identified with all who make it their business to help the stranger in need. But for the Christian disciple, it is important to note the question to which this parable was the answer: Who *is* my neighbor? The lawyer wanted to test Jesus on the question of eternal life, a benefit for which anyone could reasonably be expected to fulfill all necessary obligations. So the logic of his question was impeccable. Clearly he could not regard everyone as his neighbor. Whom, then, should he make arrangements to love?

His question revealed his failure to grasp the commandment Jesus had just advised him to keep. In the same way, the disciples missed the point when they asked Jesus whether a sevenfold forgiveness of a brother was adequate. Jesus' answer on that occasion was much the same: Seventy times seven—and keep counting (Matt. 18:22).

Our problem with neighborly relations does not lie so much with a limited perspective on people and their needs. Global bad manners are endemic to the human race, and Christians must learn to improve in this area no less than everyone else. For disciples of Jesus Christ, the problem lies rather with a parochial and limited view of God's righteousness. If we are to understand the purpose of our discipleship, we must never forget that the weight of Jesus' message was inclusive, not exclusive. Never mind *who* believes, *no one* is excluded from the love of God in Christ.

. To obey the One who has called us to discipleship, therefore, global good manners are not enough. We must love the whole world, to the point of laying down our lives for Christ's little ones, whoever and wherever they might be. If Jesus so loved the world as to dwell in it and die for it; if the Spirit of God so loves the world as to live in the stench of filthy slums, in the agony of torture chambers, in the pain of disease and the degradation of injustice; if God so loves the world that even a sparrow in distress touches the divine parental instinct; then those of us who seek after God's righteousness must likewise view the whole world as God's family, and accordingly the whole world as our neighbor.

Seeking and Doing

That is God's blueprint for the kingdom of heaven, to the extent that we are given access to a blueprint at all. And for the Christian disciple, those are most assuredly the guidelines. The dialectic of seeking God's will and then doing it must be grasped and held in constant tension.

The ethical quality of God's justice cannot be separated from its righteous imperative, which demands a clear bias toward the poor and the helpless. God's righteousness and justice will always subsume ethical principle with the exigencies of immediate need.

Take, for example, the scandal that confronts the world daily in the late twentieth century, as fifty thousand human beings die from hunger each twenty-four hours. Ethically, we know this is wrong. The question then becomes, What can we do about it? We know that long-term solutions must be considered, ranging from education in modern agriculture to economic distribution of land and resources. But the disciple knows something more than this: that God's righteousness is offended *here and now* by the suffering of these little ones, and that God's justice demands they be fed, *here and now*. The answer of the disciple cannot be, "Lord, when did we see thee hungry?" It can only be, "Lord, forgive us for what we do not do." If, that is, our relationship with the God of righteousness and justice, the God of Jesus Christ, is to have any integrity at all.[15]

The tension of discipleship is a constant quest, not only for the will of God, but also for the relationship with God to which Jesus invites all who will accept his call. This much the rich young ruler and the young lawyer can teach us: They both sought that quality of eternal life which can only be found in knowing the One who is the source of all life. The imperatives of God's justice and righteousness cannot be abstracted from knowing God; and the authority of God's call will always subsume principled righteousness and justice with particular tasks to be performed at particular times and in particular places. The immediacy of this relationship can never be compromised: It can only be accepted or rejected, as the lawyer and the rich young ruler discovered.

Agapē *Freedom*

It is in the Gospel according to John, and especially in chapters 13 to 17, that Jesus plumbs the depths of this relationship with his disciples. One of today's most profound reflections on these discourses remains Frederick Herzog's ground-breaking *Liberation Theology*, in which he defines the discipleship Jesus created as a new community for freedom, a counter-church.[16] It is a community that draws its very lifeblood from God's *agapē* love. Thus, when Jesus takes a bowl of water and washes the disciples' feet (John 13:2-11), Herzog observes:

> We would misunderstand Jesus' deed if we would regard it only as the
> deed of a good man. Service is not distinctively Christian. It is a universal
> human trait expressing the intensity of one's commitment to the family
> of man. Jesus' service is distinct as embodiment of corporate selfhood
> intending to reflect the *agapē* of God. . . . By washing the disciples' feet
> no leper was healed, no hunger stilled, no thirst quenched. . . . He
> almost seems to say: do the absurd. But upon closer examination we
> realize that he is offering a dramatic sign by which we can remember the
> point of his work. It is all about *servanthood at the boundary of life* where no
> one else cares. "The Son of man is come to save that which was lost"
> (Matt. 18:11). . . . As one searches the Fourth Gospel for specific events
> in which Jesus directly expresses his love for his disciples one looks in
> vain. Only indirectly does it become clear what his love was: he loved his
> disciples in letting them share in his identification with the lost.[17]

As the discourses proceed, Jesus unfolds for the disciples that the
closer they are to him, the closer they are to God. The more they get to
know him, the more they know God (John 14:8-14, 16:25-33). This is
the authority and power of their call. But the God they come to know
reveals increasingly the bias of a justice and righteousness that will
surely impel the disciples to share in the work of God among the poor
and the helpless. In this they will know *agapē*, the love of God with
which they will also be able to love one another (John 14:15, 23f.).

It is in the final discourses, however, that Jesus shares with his
disciples the full extent of his ministry among them, and how much he
is entrusting to them (John 16 and 17). The purpose of his earthly life
will culminate in his passion and death, and in this too they must learn
to follow him. The account in the Synoptics is more succinct, and even
more direct. Following Peter's confession at Caesarea Philippi, Jesus
begins to explain to the disciples that he will suffer, be killed, and be
raised on the third day. They cannot accept that this will happen, and
Jesus' reply to Peter, "Get thee behind me Satan," is a warning for all
true disciples. We must be so at one with the will of God that even the
concern of closest friends and companions is not allowed to intervene
(Matt. 16:21-24; Mark 8:31-39; Luke 9:22-27).

Agapē *Surrender*

Jesus goes on to make clear that being his disciple may even require
the laying down of one's life; for to take up one's cross in those days

could mean only one thing (Matt. 16:24-26; Luke 14:27). Discipleship, in the deepest sense of the word, means a complete surrender to the will of God, a giving back to God of everything we have received, including our very lives. This is not to say that we should therefore seek martyrdom: This may or may not be God's will for us. But we should be ready for any sacrifice whatsoever, in complete obedience to Christ.

That the first disciples were not ready for such a complete sacrifice is of course well known from the passion narratives in the Gospels. Even so, they were granted the supreme privilege of being witnesses to Christ's resurrection from the dead—though the women who had followed Jesus were the first to be so honored (Matt. 28:1ff., 16ff.; Mark 16:1ff.; Luke 24:1ff.; John 20:1ff.). Their subsequent empowerment at Pentecost, and their boldness in accepting the cost of their witness to the risen Christ, were to lay the foundations of authentic Christian discipleship thereafter: a sharing in the complete self-surrender of Jesus to the will of God, if need be unto death; and a sharing in his resurrection, inaugurally here and now in the presence of the Holy Spirit, and for all eternity at his coming again.

The Early Church

It is clear from the Acts of the Apostles that it was just this sort of discipleship which proved to be the bedrock of the early church. Certainly the word *disciple* is used time and again of the entire body of believers in Jesus Christ, and thus identifies all members of the primitive Christian community.[18] We find the disciples "increasing in number" in Jerusalem (Acts 6:1, 7), and the twelve summoning the "body of the disciples" in order to select the seven who would serve at tables in the daily distribution to the needy (Acts 6:2). Following Saul's conversion, his hosts in Damascus are described as disciples, as is Ananias, who ministered to him (Acts 9:10, 19). And when he returns to Jerusalem, the Christian community, again described as disciples, are suspicious of Saul because they do not at first believe he is a disciple, the accepted identity of a Christian (Acts 9:26).

The reason for this collective identification of the primitive Christian community as disciples is quite straightforward: That is precisely what they were. Becoming a Christian in those early days of the church required a radical change in a person's self-understanding and social environment both.[19] In part this was because conversion to Christianity most often came through personal contact, and thus affected people much more deeply than would have been the case in more formal settings. It was also due to the intimacy of their meetings, as can readily be inferred from the following description of these early Christian communities:

> A typical Christian cell was normally small, limited by the physical capacity of the house in which it met. The owner of the house functioned as host or patron; his or her name often was used as identification (Acts 18:7-8; Rom. 16:23; I Cor. 1:16; Col. 4:15). The group was organized on determinedly egalitarian lines. The early Christian in Jerusalem practiced community ownership of property (Acts 2:44-47). Women played as prominent a role as men. Slaves and freed men and women shared equally with the freeborn. Within the group, at least in the early decades, there was a conscious rejection of the status-conscious norms of society, a rejection summarized in the admonition that within the community of the baptized there was "neither Jew nor Greek . . . slave nor free . . . male nor female." (Gal. 3:28; cf. James 2:2-12)[20]

The House Ekklēsia

The word they used to describe their gatherings, *ekklēsia*, was the common Greek term for any kind of assembly. Translated "church," it has become the most common description of the Christian community. These disciples were careful, of course, to distinguish themselves from other *ekklēsiai*, or gatherings, by declaring that they were the people of God, gathered in the name of Jesus Christ. Paul's salutations at the opening of his letters are a good illustration of this (I Cor. 1:2f., etc.).

The gatherings seem for the most part to have been in houses, judging from the references throughout the Acts of the Apostles and the Pauline epistles. The house of Mary, mother of John Mark, for example, is identified as a place where many gathered together for prayer (Acts 12:12). After Pentecost, they attended the temple daily, but broke bread in their homes (Acts 2:46). When Saul took part in their persecution, he entered "house after house," dragging off men and women to prison (Acts 8:3). When Lydia was converted, her household was baptized with her (Acts 16:15). And for two years in Rome, Paul lived in his own hired dwelling, "preaching the kingdom of God and teaching about the Lord Jesus Christ quite openly and unhindered" (Acts 28:30).

There is discussion among students of these house churches about whether they adopted a patriarchal or egalitarian form of association.[21]

But one thing can certainly be inferred from studies of small groups in our own day and age: On the premise that human beings have not changed all that much in their basic social characteristics, these house churches must have had a tendency to develop a cohesiveness which focused their members on similar issues and ideas. By the same token, they must also have evinced a strong pressure on newcomers to accept their existing norms.[22] In other words, to join the early church was not merely to become an adherent; for even the social structure of the *ekklēsia* ensured that new members became disciples of Jesus Christ in a very intentional way.

Whither, Then, Discipleship?

The question we raised in the opening chapter therefore comes back with renewed cogency: Why does the church of today not evince similar commitment and spiritual power? Why has Christian discipleship become such a loose word? One answer of course lies in the evolution of the church from small charismatic gatherings in Christian houses to the religious institutions of Christendom. Central to this is the conversion of the Roman emperor Constantine in the year 312, leading to the Edict of Milan in 313, which extended toleration and property rights to Christians, and thence to the first great ecumenical council of the church at Nicaea in 325, which the emperor himself convened. The transition of Christianity from minority status in the empire to officially sanctioned state religion thus ensured the institutional continuity of the church; and also, as with any social structure, the necessity for its continual reform.

This does not answer the deeper question, however, of how and why the charismatic and sacrificial discipleship of the early house churches did not prevail. If Jesus did in fact inaugurate a new family, a new household, a new reign of God on earth as in heaven, then why did these first disciples, imbued with the authority and power of the Holy Spirit, not multiply indefinitely? Why did the Christianizing of the Roman Empire not mark the quantum leap into the reign of God many in the church anticipated? Why instead did the fall of Rome to Gothic pagans in the year 412 cause Augustine of Hippo and others to look for alternative visions of the kingdom of God, and establish the spiritualized dichotomy between things temporal and things eternal which has subsequently dominated so much of Christian thought?

Some observers answer this question by recommending a return to the form and the substance of primitive Christianity. William J. Abraham, for example, has recently argued for more thorough initiation into the spiritual conditions and moral obligations of Christian discipleship as the most promising way of building an authentic evangelism for our time. He stresses that this is not initiation into the church *per se*, but into the kingdom of God, another plane of existence, of which the church is the proleptic community. The implications of this initiation for local congregations are a return to the criteria for membership of the early church: conversion, baptism, morality, credal beliefs, spiritual gifts, and spiritual disciplines. To the extent that congregations fail to initiate their members into these privileges and responsibilities, they lack the authority and the spiritual signs and wonders of the early Christian communities.[23]

Imminent Expectations

It can also be argued, however, that the adherence of the early church to the teachings of Jesus, their commitment to God's righteousness and justice and love of neighbor, and even the power of their preaching to call others to conversion, were all strengthened by their firm expectation that his promises would be fulfilled in his imminent return in glory. In that New Testament disciples were to a large degree motivated and empowered by the belief that Jesus was indeed the Messiah, this not only led them to accept their spiritual gifts as normative of the inaugurated reign of God. It also sustained them in a life-style which quickly earned them harassment and persecution, which was often sacrificial, but which they accepted willingly as of imminently short duration.

This is nowhere more in evidence than in the Pauline corpus. In I Thessalonians, probably his earliest letter, written around the year 51 when he was in Corinth, Paul describes the return of Christ in language that has an inescapable immediacy. The Thessalonians have turned from their idols to serve God, "and to wait for his Son from heaven" (1:10). Other references throughout the letter (2:19, 3:13, 5:23) culminate in the famous passage where he warns them to be ready for the day of the Lord, which will come "like a thief in the night," with "the archangel's call, and with the sound of the trumpet of God" (4:13–15:11).[24]

In subsequent writings, Paul lessens his sense of immediacy, as in his letter to the Philippians, where he has clearly come to accept that the *parousia* may not come in his lifetime (1:23). But elsewhere, in Romans (8:18, 13:11f.), I Corinthians (15:20-26, 51-53), Colossians (3:4), and other places, his hope in the reality of Christ's return is undiminished. References in the four Gospels are also sufficiently substantial to "confirm the view that the parousia expectation was vital to the early church and that it originated in the teachings of Jesus."[25]

How, then, did they sustain their discipleship when the promises of Christ seemed less and less likely to be fulfilled as they hoped? How did they retain the commitment of their ecclesial communities when many of their converts, to say nothing of they themselves, had been won through preaching that announced a forthcoming event which seemed to be repeatedly postponed?

These are of course questions we ought to be asking today in the church with much more frequency and intentionality. And the reason we do not ask them is that we have found ways of avoiding the urgency of proclaiming the return of Christ. We have adopted a gospel that neglects to announce the fulfillment of the reign of God—which is to say that we have a very truncated version of the gospel indeed.

Eschatological Dimensions

As Geoffrey Wainwright reminds us in his definitive volume, *Eucharist and Eschatology*, these matters have been much more on our theological agenda in the twentieth century than once was the case. Since the work of Johannes Weiss and Albert Schweitzer at the turn of this century, there have been a number of approaches to eschatology, which Wainwright classifies under "vertical" and "horizontal" dimensions:

> The eternal invades time in a moment, the supernatural breaks into the natural, the heavenly bursts upon the earthly scene, and at each moment the individual may be confronted with final judgment. Yet time goes on: the parousia of Christ is still awaited, we are not yet in our resurrection bodies, the perfect community does not yet rejoice together in the unclouded vision of God.[26]

Both dimensions are necessary to understand the radical immanence of the Christ event in human history, but also the radically unfulfilled promises of the coming reign of God.

Ever since the early church came to accept that Christ might not return as soon as they had hoped, Christian discipleship has inexorably been a question of living faithfully and hopefully, a stance of active expectancy. For once it became clear that children were going to be born and old people were going to die much as before; and once it became necessary to transcribe the teachings of Jesus into written form, and then to wrestle with all the questions of canonical selection and ecclesial authority; and once it became clear that churches, just like other social institutions, could be a very mixed grouping indeed; then the full implications of Jesus' teachings began to affect the collective Christian memory.

The prophetic tradition of the Old Testament, with its vision of universal *shalom*, extending not only to all peoples and nations, but also to all forms of life on planet Earth, was remembered as something Jesus had affirmed. The parables of Jesus, in which he spoke about seed, and light, and leaven and salt, began to have relevance to the organic life of the church, much of which involved the hard work and ambivalent results of community building as well as the crisis of persecution and martyrdom. But most important of all, the universal saving-righteousness of God was aligned with the particularities of divine justice, to provide a setting for Christian discipleship in a work of salvation which had awesome cosmic dimensions of grace.

Primitive Faithfulness

It has been one of the most unfortunate and persistent mistakes of the church not to take note of this remarkable act of faith on the part of the early church. They could have returned to the old Hebrew tradition, and consigned Jesus of Nazareth to their long line of prophets. They could just as easily have become a Jewish messiah movement, withdrawing into an enclave of other-worldly anticipation (which, of course, some of them did).[27] Instead, they took the beliefs and hopes of the Hebrew tradition, and gave them a bold new meaning in light of the death and resurrection of Jesus. They proclaimed that God had entered into human history uniquely, unilaterally, and unequivocally; that the world had entered into a new age, and would never be the same again.

But they also declared that this did not negate the Jewish tradition. The history of Yahweh remained in place, with the accumulated wisdom of discerning, trusting, and obeying this very active God. The righteousness of Yahweh remained in place, with laws of immutable justice for the poor and oppressed. The promises of Yahweh remained in place, with the vision of a new heaven and a new earth, for which Christians would have to wait with the same patience as the Jews.

Inaugural Birthpangs

The true significance of the Christ event lay in the inaugural birthpangs of a new earthly order which would emerge as laboriously as all other earthly births, but which would be equally awesome in its fulfillment. And the privilege of being a Christian was the commission to announce that message to the world with the full authority and power of the Holy Spirit.

Christian discipleship, therefore, in its pristine connotation, was not limited to the twelve who followed Jesus. It was the accepted identity of the entire Christian community, extending from Jerusalem to the missionary churches of Paul. By definition, it entailed countercultural beliefs and a countercultural life-style of active expectancy of the coming reign of God. It meant joining with the risen Christ in confronting the powers and principalities of this world, wherever they held sway. It meant announcing with the power of the Holy Spirit that God's righteousness would ultimately prevail, on earth as in heaven. And it meant accepting responsibility, not only for sustaining ecclesial communities of active expectancy, but also for ensuring that the task was duly handed on to the next generation of faithful disciples.

Discipleship and Salvation

The universality of this message, however, and the particularity of this identity, point us toward a distinction we will ultimately find to be unavoidable. For if Christ died for all the world, yet discipleship in its pristine form has not been practiced throughout the church, then we must surely ask whether discipleship and salvation are the same thing. Addressing this question may well be the answer to our North American dilemma.

UNIVERSAL GRACE: THE COMING REIGN OF GOD

Heraldic Messengers

Once we realize that an expectation of the imminent return of Christ was integral to the gospel message of the early church, the task of Christian discipleship emerges with new cogency and clarity. In a word, Christian disciples are first and foremost heraldic messengers. Their message is an announcement, the Good News that Jesus Christ is the Savior of the world, and that God intends to make this a universal reality with the return of Christ in glory. This means seeing the world as the planet God has promised to save. It means confronting the world with the need for repentance and conversion to God's righteousness. It also means reaching out to the world with the compassion of Christ, and with all the empathy of human beings, who are as much a part of this creation as every other creature that inhabits the earth. Jesus made clear that this was God's parental concern, and that nothing less was required of his disciples (Matt. 6:26-28, 10:29; Luke 12:6f., 24, 27).

What he did not make clear, however, was how long it would take for this salvation to come to pass, and how many generations of faithful disciples would have to inherit and pass on the heraldic task. The spontaneous announcement of the *evangel* was of course a mark of the church from its Pentecostal baptism onward. But the primary concern of Christian disciples in those earliest days was to be ready for God's salvation to come to dramatic fulfillment with the return of Christ. The extent to which they would be involved in getting others to share their expectancy became clear to them only as the delay in this

56

parousia persisted, and as the missionary work of Paul and others to the Gentiles revealed the scope and the potential of their evangelistic responsibilities.

As a result, the underlying concern of Christian disciples soon became, and has remained across the centuries, the sustaining of their identity; and this involves considerable hard work. It might seem a little ponderous to describe the keeping of one's identity as toilsome; but for the Christian disciple, that is exactly what it is. The delayed *parousia* means that Christians must live in the constant tension of particular faith and global humanity. They expect the return of Christ, yet they continue to live in the world like every other human being. In every generation, they must work at discerning, proclaiming, and living out the particularity of the Christian message, yet they cannot deny their responsibility to human existence or future. Indeed, association with the human race and participation in the life of planet Earth is the very significance of their incarnational gospel.

Particular and Universal

As with any situation where there are dialectical responsibilities, it is always possible to ease the tension by opting for one or the other. Thus, when Christian identity becomes problematic rather than challenging, as in our present dilemma of discipleship, it is usually because Christians have attempted to circumvent this polarity of particular and universal. The result is either a dogmatic Christian message which has lost its relevance to human existence, or a compromised Christian tradition which has lost its capacity to address the human condition.

Christians who opt for the particularity of the gospel message tend to make their salvation a parochial, even an exclusive concept, and seek their identity by withdrawing from the world. Interestingly enough, this is rarely the case with the monastic orders of the church, or the various radical movements which emerge to reform the church from time to time. These may give the impression of withdrawal, but their involvement in the world is by and large all the more intentional because of their spiritually disciplined life-styles. The examples are rather to be found among those churchgoers who perceive themselves to have privileged status with God by virtue of their beliefs. Their withdrawal from the world is usually highly subjective, and almost always inconsistent; for seldom do they allow the qualitative difference they place between themselves and their fellow human beings to deprive them of the necessities or comforts of worldly living.

By the same token, the tension of Christian discipleship can be relieved by opting for the universality of the gospel to the neglect or even the denial of its scandalous particularity. In the sphere of congregational life, the most common evidence of this is an accommodating folk religion which avoids the challenge of Christian witness to the world. As we have already noted, this has been a persistent tendency in contemporary North American Protestantism, where a civil religion propounded by church and state alike blurs the focus of Christian proclamation. Unwilling to enter into a relationship with God distinct from that of American culture, the church attempts instead to impose a sacred interpretation on the secular, refusing to accept that the secular is also under God's sovereignty and therefore inherently valid. In so doing, the church loses its authority; because the secular, while accepting a certain degree of sacralization, does not regard the church as having more or less significance than any other social structure.[1]

Thus it is hardly surprising, though regrettable nonetheless, that much of the North American church of today reacts to such social disdain by yielding to the cultural norms of instant satisfaction and hedonistic self-fulfillment. With supreme irony, as the world trembles on the brink of unprecedented cosmic discoveries, Christian discipleship is reduced to little more than the realization of human personhood. The awesome dimensions of God's creation are blithely ceded to the mathematical sciences, and the deepest mysteries of God's salvation willingly consigned to psychiatric counseling. Writing against the backdrop of the 1976 Bicentennial of the United States, Richard John Neuhaus had this to say:

> The church needs rather an imaginative re-appropriation of its own tradition, a theological recovery of nerve, a new confidence to live in dialectic with the larger culture, an unembarrassed readiness to affirm the scandal of its particularity. Only such a church can "save its own soul."[2]

The Particularity of Christ

It is when the church truly appropriates this tradition that the tension of its identity becomes inescapable. For the particular Christ event reveals nothing less than the universality of God's saving-righteousness. The Christian must wrestle with this dialectic, plumb the depths of its mysteries, and unfailingly proclaim its Good News to the world:

> Jesus, the name high over all
> In hell, or earth, or sky;
> Angels and men before it fall,
> And devils fear and fly.
>
> · · · · ·
>
> O that the world might taste and see
> The riches of his grace!
> The arms of love that compass me
> Would all mankind embrace.
>
> · · · · ·
>
> Happy, if with my latest breath
> I may but gasp his name!
> Preach him to all, and cry in death,
> "Behold! behold the Lamb."[3]

The Christ event is of course particular because of its grounding in the Judaic tradition. But more than that, it is historical and specific. Jesus of Nazareth died on the cross while Pontius Pilate was governor of Judea. Most important of all, he was raised from the dead while Pilate was still governor, and appeared to his followers in order to commission them for their evangelistic mission throughout the world.

These particularities immediately place the Christian in a confrontation with things the way they are. To begin with, they give a whole new significance to time. While the human race finds meaning primarily through the cyclical myths of existence, which impose memories onto the past and project hopes onto the future, the Christian finds meaning in a particular historical event. Far from being shaped by present memory and hope, this Christ event reshapes the whole of human existence, past, present, and future. As Mircea Eliade has put it, those who stand in the Judeo-Christian tradition are creatures of time—but historical time:

> Judaism presents an innovation of the first importance. For Judaism, time has a beginning and will have an end. . . . Christianity goes even further in valorizing *historical time*. Since God was *incarnated*, that is,

since he took on a *historically conditioned human existence,* history acquires the possibility of being sanctified. The *illud tempus* evoked by the Gospels is a clearly defined historical time—the time in which Pontius Pilate was Governor of Judea—but it was *sanctified by the presence of Christ.* When a Christian of our day participates in liturgical time, he recovers the *illud tempus* in which Christ lived, suffered, and rose again—but it is no longer a mythical time, it is the time when Pontius Pilate governed Judea.[4]

All of this gives the Christian a very particular identity indeed, and one that cannot be effortlessly sustained in a world where human ideals, or more often human exigencies, govern concepts of reality—a world that has not yet accepted the divine reality that God was in Christ.

The Universality of the Gospel

Over against this particularity there is the universal significance of the Christ event. Jesus came with God's forgiveness and reconciliation for all the world (John 3:16), commissioned his disciples to take it to all the world (Matt. 28:18-20), and gave them the spiritual gifts and power to do so (Acts 2:1-4). This was his vision from the very beginning, as he made clear when he announced his public ministry by reading from the most universal of all the Old Testament prophets:

> The Spirit of the Lord is upon me,
> because he has anointed me to preach good news to the poor.
> He has sent me to proclaim release to the captives
> and recovering of sight to the blind,
> to set at liberty those who are oppressed,
> to proclaim the acceptable year of the Lord.
>
> (Luke 4:18-19; cf. Isa. 61:1-2)

The dramatic significance of Jesus' announcement in the Nazareth synagogue was that this vision had come to pass in the very hearing of his audience. His words carried the power, not only of future promise, but also of a present breaking in of the salvation which will one day come to fulfillment. *Now* is the time of love and justice and peace. *Now* is the acceptable year of the Lord. *Now* is the year of Jubilee.[5]

The Kingdom of God

These prophetic words are an overture of the theme which dominates the teaching and preaching of Jesus—the *basileia*. Variously termed the kingdom (Luke 12:32), the kingdom of God (Mark 1:15), the kingdom of heaven (Matt. 5:3), or the kingdom of the Father (Matt. 13:43), it signifies a state of monarchy, of royal rule. To describe it as the "realm" of God is not enough, for this Kingdom is not just a place, albeit with spatial, existential, historical, or eschatological attributes. It is the reign of God: a new age of love and justice and peace, and with a ruler. Moreover, the ruler has been named: Jesus, the carpenter's son, from Nazareth (Luke 1:33; Matt. 13:41; John 18:36). Any attempt therefore to equate the kingdom of God with a social perfecting of worldly systems is to engage in what Jürgen Moltmann has described as presumptive utopianism.[6] It is to usurp the divine prerogative, and history is littered with such abortive attempts.

On the other hand, just as there are mistaken attempts to objectify this coming new age by divorcing it from the personal rule of Jesus Christ, so there is a tendency, fostered by generations of Protestant theology and reinforced by the present individualism of North American culture, to subjectify it as a religious state of mind, or a spiritual plane of existence. This is frequently derived from a marginal reading of Luke 17:21, "the kingdom of God is within you," a reading that seems to be corroborated by other texts. There are places, for example, where Jesus variously describes the Kingdom as a gift (Luke 12:32, Matt. 21:43), or a possession (Matt. 5:3, 10). As might be expected, this subjective approach views the wider dimensions of the reign of God as the social, global, and ultimately eternal aggregate of those who are Christ-minded, Kingdom-gifted, and Spirit-filled. The implication is that personal conversions must therefore be the priority of the church's evangelistic ministry, for this is how the reign of God will come to pass: a process of accumulative and selective augmentation, culminating in a *parousia* of mutual recognition.

We shall address this weighty error in greater detail when we come to examine its corollary, the mistaken use of the doctrine of reprobation. But for the present, we can note that a more accurate reading of Luke 17:21 is "the kingdom is among you," or "in your midst."[7] The point of Christ's reply to the Pharisees in this context is to declare that apocalyptic signs and wonders are not necessary to validate the Kingdom. He himself is its validation, its embodiment. It is a reality here and now because God's love is a reality; the righteousness of God's justice is a reality here and now, embodied in Christ, who is Jesus the Jew.

A New Age: The Coming Reign of God

The question, therefore, is not whether people opt for the Kingdom, but whether they acknowledge it.[8] Its fulfillment does not lie in the aggregate of those who cry "Lord, Lord," but in the actualization of its axioms among *all* people (Matt. 7:21-23; Luke 6:46; John 13:13-15). It is a reordering of the whole of humanity, a new age *(palingenesia)*, in which the poor will be cared for, and those with great wealth will distribute it to the needy—in short, where the first will be last and the last first (Matt. 19:16-30). And all of this to fulfill what M. Douglas Meeks has termed "God's economy of righteousness."[9]

This reordering, in which the justice of God's righteousness will exalt the humble and meek, the merciful, and the peacemakers, will not, however, come without a struggle. Beelzebul, the prince of demons, is identified as the ruler of a rival kingdom (Matt. 12:25; Mark 3:24; Luke 11:17f.), and Jesus is the first to recognize that his Kingdom is in direct confrontation with present worldly powers. Indeed, the use of the same word *basileia* to connote the kingdoms the devil offers to Jesus during his temptation is an indication, not only of the scope of the new age, but also of the conflict which will be necessary before it is fulfilled (Matt. 4:8; Luke 4:5). There will be a purging of all that is evil (Matt. 13:41), and nothing less than a complete transformation: a new heaven and a new earth (Rev. 21:1). The eternal reality will be the kingdom of God, not the kingdoms of this world; which, as Jesus declares before Pilate, are of a different order altogether (John 18:36). The Pilates of this world hold transitory power at best. Jesus will reign for ever and ever (Rev. 11:15).

The radical difference between the kingdoms of this world and the coming reign of God is important to keep in mind because of the limitations implicit in our contemporary use of kingly metaphors. Monarchies are rare in the world of today, and those remaining are strictly limited in their role. Moreover, the symbols of power associated with kingdoms have been the source of much oppression across the ages, a great deal of it masculine oppression. It is of utmost significance, therefore, that this Kingdom is the work of God, and not of human beings, as Jesus is at pains to stress (Matt. 25:34; Mark 4:26-29; Luke 12:32). It is self-evident to those with eyes to see and ears to hear, but its coming is ultimately a mystery—as, for that matter, is the evil and suffering which presently hinder its realization (Matt. 13:24-30; Mark 4:30-32; Luke 13:20f.). All of these things are in God's hands, and not even Jesus knows the day or the hour when the new age will be ushered in in its fullness (Matt. 24:36). We are to expect it, imminently, and we are to pray for it without ceasing—"Thy kingdom come; Thy will be done, On earth as in heaven" (Matt. 6:10)—but we must never presume to predict the time or the manner of its advent. God's calendar and God's strategy are divinely privileged information.

A New Order: The Economy of God

And so the New Testament, gathering up the promises of the Hebrew scriptures, proclaims this Good News *(eyangelion)* of the early church: A new age is coming, when time and eternity will be fused into a glorious new creation (Rev. 21:1-4); when there will be neither Jew nor Greek, neither slave nor free, neither male nor female (Gal. 3:28); when the wolf shall dwell with the lamb, the leopard shall lie down with the kid, the lion shall eat straw like the ox, and the earth shall be as full of the knowledge of God as there are waters that cover the sea (Isa. 11:8ff.); when everyone will know God, from the least to the greatest (Jer. 31:34). A new order is coming, *oikonomia tou theou*, when justice will roll down like waters, and righteousness like an ever-flowing stream (Amos 5:24); when there will be no more sound of weeping, nor cries of distress; when all children shall live beyond infancy, and all old people shall live out their days; when those who build houses shall live in them, not others; when those who plant vineyards shall eat of them, and not others (Isa. 65:20-25).

This announcement is nothing if not urgent. God has a plan of salvation for the world that involves some very radical changes, where suffering, injustice, and poverty will be no more. The implications for those of us who call ourselves Christians are therefore inescapable. *If we have accepted a place in this plan of salvation: if we have been reconciled to God in Christ; if we claim to be disciples of the crucified and risen Jew;* then the message he announced that day in the synagogue at Nazareth, the message he deliberately traditioned from the prophecies of God's justice and righteousness, must be *our message also.* And we must announce it with the same urgency. For the day is coming when the whole of creation will be a new *oikos,* God's new household, "for whose redemption (ultimate livelihood) God as its Economist has become responsible through God's promises."[10]

Credit Card Christians

It is possible, of course, to spiritualize these promises and relegate them to a heavenly realm, thereby consigning this world to a permanent state of inadequacy and ultimate hopelessness. But that is to give disparate meaning to the teaching and the prophetic preaching of Jesus. As Mortimer Arias has explained, it is to apply the gospel *about* Jesus to this world, but to consign the gospel *of* Jesus to the next.[11] It is to accept the benefits of God's saving-righteousness here and now, but regard its responsibilities as incidental, and virtually impossible to exercise in the world as it is. It is to view one's salvation as rescue *out of* the world, rather than as a privilege to be shared *with* the world. In late-twentieth-century North American practice, it is to put our obligations to Jesus Christ, our considerable obligations, on a credit card.

The only way to engage in our discipleship with integrity is to take the whole of the gospel and, as faithful messengers, proclaim the truthfulness of Christ's promises as well as his teachings. We are to announce this new age, and trust in the work of the Holy Spirit to give our announcement power and conviction. Moreover, we are to live according to these promises, giving the world a clear sign that the new age has begun. It is not merely that the habits of the old age are wrong. They are patently out of date. The new age has come, for there are those who are already living in it. And one day, soon, this new age will be universal.

The Promises of Christ

More than anything else, it is the open future of the gospel message, looking to the fulfillment of Christ's promises in his *parousia*, that ultimately governs the identity of our discipleship. It means for one thing that, as Christians, we do not have all the answers. This obvious fact is often given lip service as a truism; but its implications for discipleship need to be spelled out much more clearly in the life and work of the church. In plain words, it means that God's redemption of planet Earth is more, much more, than the salvation of individuals. It means that God's salvation in Christ cannot and must not be reduced to piecemeal soteriological transactions. Any attempt on the part of individual Christians to announce that they are saved is altogether premature. Christians know they are going to be saved; they know they are being saved; and in one sense, a very limited sense, they have a foretaste of their salvation. But the fullness of God's salvation, the culmination of God's saving-righteousness, the new heavens and the new earth, all of these lie in the future. No one has that fullness; not yet.

And when, by contrast, even a cursory thought is given to the countless millions in the world who are hungry, who are suffering, who languish under injustice, or are ravaged by war, the prospect of anyone celebrating personal salvation becomes even less tolerable. In fact, it borders on the obscene. There are still too many of Christ's little ones who are hungry, too many who lack clothes, too many who are sick and in prison. There are still too many empty places at the *parousia* banquet table. The appropriate attitude for guests who have already arrived, therefore, is to nibble on the appetizers (the "firstfruits"), and anticipate the feast which is to come. To sit down and begin to eat would be an unpardonable lapse of good manners, especially since the host is out looking for the missing guests, and could certainly use some help.

Election by God

There are those who feel that to argue for such a universal interpretation of the gospel reduces the particularity of Christian discipleship, much as the Pharisees opposed Jesus for his alleged weakening of the Jewish law. When we explore the roots of universal salvation in the scriptures, however, we find quite the opposite. The identity of Israel, and that of new Israel, the church, proves to be every bit as distinctive as we have suggested, but never at the expense of the rest of the world. Their election, their chosenness, is always that of being called into a particular relationship with God for the purpose of proclaiming a universal message.

We find this in the very roots of the Judaic tradition. As Paul reminds us, Christian identity is grounded in the spiritual history of Israel and their election as the chosen people of Yahweh (Gal. 3:29). Even though it came into use theologically at a comparatively late date, the idea of their election, the belief that they were Yahweh's special people, goes back to the earliest Hebrew tradition. It is highly significant, therefore, that Abraham's response in obedience to God, the pivotal moment in the history of Israel's election, has a universal purpose. God calls Abraham, and promises to make of him a great nation, in order to be a blessing to all the families of the earth (Gen. 12:1-3).[12]

Although this concept of election is implicit in the earliest documents of the Pentateuch, it is in the Yahwist presentation that the stories of the various traditions are first taken and fashioned into God's saving history. The concept is both wide and deep. It is wide, in that God chooses Abraham so that through Israel salvation might come to the whole world. Each event is then placed in the context of God's saving-righteousness, and God's grace to Israel is shown to be something which concerns the whole human race.[13] The concept is deep, in that the relationship between Yahweh and the Israelites is intensely personal. Yahweh thinks out loud (Gen. 8:12-22); Yahweh identifies very closely with the earth (Gen. 9:6-7); and Yahweh engages in genuine dialogue (Gen. 18:22ff.). There is a sense of fearless, direct encounter with the deity, a deity so accessible as to seem almost vulnerable.[14]

Election for the World

In the eighth-century prophets, and in Second-Isaiah, we have already seen this dialectic brought into sharper focus. The will of the God who has called a particular people into a distinctive relationship is that their special knowledge must be shared with all peoples:

> Thus says God, the Lord,
>   who created the heavens and stretched them out,
>   who spread forth the earth and what comes from it,
> who gives breath to the people upon it
>   and spirit to those who walk in it:
> "I am the Lord, I have called you in righteousness,
>   I have taken you by the hand and kept you;
> I have given you as a covenant to the people,
>   a light to the nations,
>   to open the eyes that are blind,
> to bring out the prisoners from the dungeon,
>   from the prison those who sit in darkness."
>   (Isa. 42:5-7)

Only in and through this mission to the world can Israel fulfill the purpose of God's election; an election, not of particular privilege, but of universal responsibility. It is the ground of their identity as the people of God, both as servants and as messengers, and proves to be a source of deep enrichment for their inheritance.[15] Their election by God is to be interpreted as service, discipline, and accountability. It is by no means a call to superiority. For not only is the choice of Israel a mystery, as a people of little account, but also they can expect to be singled out by God as those from whom more is expected than from other peoples (Deut. 7:6-9; Amos 3:2, 9:7).

Covenant Obedience

The continuing basis of Israel's relationship with Yahweh is the Sinai covenant (Deut. 5:2ff.). It is entered into freely, a response to God's gracious acts toward the Israelites, and it has to be renewed voluntarily by each generation. Yet it is not unconditional. Even though the predominant nature of the covenant is God's grace, and the initiative remains with God, there are commandments to be obeyed. It is in the appropriation of Yahweh's will that the covenant is to be lived out; and though obedience is not a prerequisite of the relationship, it is an obligation of continuing in it. When Israel fails to accept this obligation, it is made clear that they are thereby repudiating God's election (Isa. 1:2, 4; Jer. 18:1ff.; Hos. 6:7, 8:1).

This need for obedient response to God's initiative gives the covenant a worldly quality, grounded in the historical realities of God's actions. The recounting of Israel's relationship with Yahweh in the Old Testament is marked by an earthy candor. The covenant election of God is nothing if not direct; indeed, so direct that, among other responses from the Israelites, God's initiative can incur their rage. So vital is their covenant relationship with Yahweh, that they dare to believe that protest is sometimes more fitting than submission.[16]

Religious Exclusiveness

Conversely, the directness of Israel's relationship with Yahweh is weakened when the universal implications of the covenant are subsumed by its religious and theological dimensions. This first becomes evident in the Elohist tradition, as Israel is set over against the other nations of the world instead of being a means of blessing for them. God's dominion and fellowship become restricted to Israel, a perception further developed by the Deuteronomic and Priestly traditions; and, as a result, the calling of Israel becomes not one of election *for* other peoples, but selection *from* them (Num. 23:9). The world of the nations becomes the world of paganism and apostasy from Yahweh (Exod. 32:25-29). Instead of Israel being an instrument of God's salvation for the human race, specific acts of election by God are viewed primarily for cultic and kingly purposes. In the struggle against the Canaanite nature religions, election takes on an axiomatic and exclusive connotation.[17]

Perhaps this was a necessary defense against erosion by other religions. But the crucial question is posed by von Rad, who asks whether a theology which saw Israel's existence so strongly conditioned by praise of Yahweh could have strayed this far from the proper road.[18] When the people of Israel were in active and positive relationship with their God, they were truly free to proclaim salvation for the nations. But when they turned away from God, they began to cling to an exclusive identity as a form of defense, unaware that in so doing they had already weakened their covenant.

The implications for today's North American church life are weighty. A people in active, obedient covenant with God will reflect the universal purpose of God's saving-righteousness. If they reject their covenant, however, denying the righteousness of God's justice, neglecting or even spurning the poor, the hungry, and the helpless, they will have a warped view of God, a view at once more exclusive and more judgmental.

Tragically, this religious exclusiveness will also engender a failure to sense God's judgment. For the people of Israel, regarding themselves as God's people over against the nations of the world, began to look for a "Day of Yahweh," when their foes would be vanquished. They did not listen to the prophets, who warned them of their own approaching day of reckoning. "Yahweh kept knocking at their door, but they paid no heed."[19] If these words are sobering for the North American church of today, perhaps they can also be salutary.

The New Covenant in Christ

When we turn to the New Testament, the difference is not, as is often inferred, an emphasis on grace as opposed to works. Election to covenant with God is always a gracious concept in the Old Testament, with a focus on God's love—an understanding that continued in the Rabbinic religion of the intertestamental period.[20] The difference is that, instead of a righteousness coming from obedient response to God's covenant initiative, there is now a complete dependence on Christ. Obedience is still the condition of the covenant relationship, but it is Christ who brings the people of God into a new covenant. It is Christ who sustains them in their righteousness, and it is being one with Christ which affords death to sin and the promise of resurrection. The new covenant is nothing more nor less than participation in the transformation of the human race, accomplished by Jesus Christ, and to be fulfilled at his return (Eph. 1:9f., 20-23; Col. 1:19f.; II Pet. 3:13).[21]

Like the covenant election of Israel, the new covenant is a special relationship with God carrying responsibility for the world. Throughout the New Testament, the church is described as the elect of God, an election that develops out of Israel. As such, it appropriates the same principles of grace and service (Gal. 6:16; Eph. 1:14f.; I Pet. 2:9).[22] In the Pauline account of the Last Supper, for example, it is clear that God's grace is extended to all peoples (I Cor. 11:23ff.). The church is the new Israel of God, called and chosen by God; but chosen to receive, by particular grace, the commission to proclaim a message of universal hope.[23]

Universal Proclamation

That the universality of this commission was not at first understood by the church is evidenced by the Apostolic Conference, to which we have already alluded (Acts 15; Gal. 2).[24] In this confrontation between Paul and the Jerusalem church, Paul was primarily concerned with the task of proclaiming the gospel to all people without distinction, willing to become "all things to all men" (I Cor. 9:22). The church in Jerusalem was concerned more with the distinctive identity of the people of God (Gal. 2:12). The Conference drew these concerns into a dialectic: Paul the missionary showing concern for the mother church; Peter and the Jerusalem leaders acknowledging the necessity of preaching a gospel for the whole world. The concept of the servant church, which emerged from this tension, appropriates the dynamic of the Israelite covenant—the people of God elected for the nations of the world. The power of the new covenant lies in the awareness of the resurrection believers that God's saving grace is universal.

Consummate Salvation

This is brought to its consummate statement in Paul's letter to the Romans, where the full scope of God's salvation is expounded. Paul makes clear at the outset that God's righteousness has a universal claim upon creation. The wrath of heaven is revealed against all ungodliness and the wickedness of all who suppress the truth (1:18). The difference between Jew and Gentile in this regard is merely one of revelation, since all human beings are accountable for what they have done in light of what they know. Those who have the Jewish law are answerable, not for knowing it, but for obeying it; those who have the law of conscience are likewise answerable for whether they have followed it. Belief in God is not the issue, for knowledge of God is written on every human heart. The question rather is, What have human beings *done* with what they believe, in whatever measure of grace God has granted them (2:6-16)? Paul's answer is unequivocal. All have sinned: All have fallen short of God's righteousness. This is not a matter of failing a test of ethical rectitude. It is the much deeper issue of turning away from God, of rejecting God's truth (1:18-23, 2:1-16).

Universal Sin

This universality of sin is crucial to Paul's exposition. It applies to all of humanity: to Jew, to Gentile, and to Christian. It was the law which identified sin for what it is, but sin existed long before that. Sin came into the world through Adam; and through sin, death, to all the human race—even to those whose sin was not like that of Adam (5:12-14). The implication is very clear: that while sin is a universal reality, its origins are a deep mystery. Whoever Adam was, and whatever Adam did or did not do in the beginnings of humanity, something happened that has affected the whole of the human race. Determining the causes, therefore, or worse, finding the culprit and apportioning blame, is far less important than dealing with the reality. Humankind is profoundly alienated from its Creator, and continues to resist the divine will, refusing to let God be God. That is the sin against which God must pronounce judgment.

Universal Righteousness

As we have already noted, however, the nature of God's judgment is to be proactive. God judges in righteousness, dispenses righteousness, and therefore takes the initiative in dealing with sin. There are no half measures. In that sin is a universal reality, so God's saving-righteousness in Jesus Christ is universal. The logic of Paul's argument here is quite impeccable. Just as sin became universal through the fall of Adam, God's redemption in Christ is nothing less:

> As one man's trespass led to condemnation for all men, so one man's act of righteousness leads to acquittal and life for all men. For as by one man's disobedience many were made sinners, so by one man's obedience many will be made righteous. (5:18-19)

Moreover, there is no contest when it comes to the respective capabilities of Adam and Christ to influence the human race. If so much havoc has been wreaked by the sin of Adam, how much more good can be wrought through Jesus Christ, the Son of God (5:15-17). If Adam's sin could affect countless human beings, including those who have not shared in Adam's particular transgression (5:14), surely God can go one better, and justify countless human beings through the righteousness of Christ.

The implications are at once staggering and ineluctable. The whole of the world is in the birthpangs of a new creation. And with the suddenness of birth after labor the reign of God will be ushered in, when neither death, nor life, nor anything in all creation, will be able to separate us from the love of God in Christ Jesus our Lord (Rom. 8:18-25, 28-30).

Universal Redemption

The elect of God are privileged to share in the firstfruits of this new age, but by no means have they a monopoly on its benefits. For Paul proceeds to bring God's universal redemption into its sharpest focus as, with deep anguish and joy, he places his own people, the Jews, in their proper salvific role. Even the hardness of the Jews toward the new covenant, he explains, has a purpose (9:19-24). They are being used as an example, as an encouragement to others, just as God once used Pharaoh (9:14-18). It is by the present rejection of a few that the many will be drawn to forgiveness. And once this divine strategy is complete, all Israel will be saved. The Deliverer will come from Zion, and will take away their sins (11:26f.). Indeed, therein lies the deepest mystery of all: that even sin has a purpose in the knowledge and wisdom of God, who "has consigned all men to disobedience, that he may have mercy upon all" (11:13-16, 28-32).

These scriptural concepts of universal grace demonstrate convincingly that our dilemma of discipleship in North America is in fact a crisis of identity. The mission to which Christians are called is that of proclaiming the universal acts of God, and the church must look beyond itself to the will of God for the world, avoiding the false identity of defining itself at the expense of the world. Christian self-understanding must be that of election to a particular relationship with God *for* the world, not *from* it.

Privatized Faith

Yet this hardly describes the cultural and soteriological havens with which most of us are familiar today. As we have suggested at each stage of our investigation, the gospel of Jesus Christ has become a privatized faith in contemporary North America, and this in every dimension of churchly life.[25] That Schleiermacher systematized personal religion so brilliantly has been the source of much of this in our theology. This in turn has left our congregational life with minimal resistance to the erosive influences of civil and folk religions.[26] Instead of the gospel affecting the whole of human life, it has become a *cultus privatus*, with but pale reflections of the coming reign of God.

As we have also observed, this is by no means the first time that Christians have made such a mistake. Wolfhart Pannenberg has argued that in fact for most of its history the church has failed to fulfill its proper worldly role, being dominated by the Augustinian identity of a spiritual rather than a worldly manifestation of God's elective grace. This has left a religious vacuum in Western political life which has been filled across the centuries by a wide range of civil religions, many of them Christian in their character, but none of them theocentric as was the early church. Indeed, the nationalisms spawned by these civil religions have often appropriated the very sense of election the church has surrendered. The ecclesiological task is therefore quite urgent:

> It may be considered high time for the Christian churches and their theology to recognize the elements of corporate election and mission as well as of judgment in the political history of Christianity. It is urgent that they be redeemed from the ambiguities and perversions of their

alienated persistence in the form of civil religions of particular nations. A re-appropriation of the subject of historical corporate election of the people of God may also relieve the churches themselves of a narrowly ecclesiocentric perspective focusing exclusively on the church as an institution.[27]

In other words, it is time for Christians, and North American Christians in particular, to take a hard look at everything Jesus promised, and not merely those parts of his message that address their personal salvation.

Response to the Gospel: Repentance and Conversion

It is at this point, however, that a very substantial question must be addressed: the question of human response to the gospel. For even as an unduly personalized discipleship fails to take into the account the universality of God's salvation, so an unduly universalized gospel fails to take into the account the critical challenge of God's love. If God's justice and righteousness are not mere ethical concepts, then God's forgiveness and reconciliation are not mere clinical therapies. They are the initiatives of a God whose love is all-demanding and all-consuming (Rom. 8:38f.; I John 4:7-12); a God whose parental wrath consigns to the deep with millstones round their necks any who lead the divine family astray; a jealous God, whose majesty is so terrible that children of the third and even fourth generations of those who worship false gods are "visited with iniquity" (Exod. 20:4-6).

The dynamic of the gospel is not only an announcement of the new age. It is also an impelling, crucial invitation to join it, to come back home to the family of God, where everyone belongs, but where no one will be forced against their will. The message, the ministry, and the passion of Jesus Christ make clear that God's grace will always give the freedom to resist grace. Thus, while the Good News is an urgent announcement, "the kingdom is at hand" (Mark 1:14-16), it is also a call to repentance and conversion *(metanoia)*. It is a call that must be made as often as possible, to as many as possible, in as many ways as possible (Matt. 4:23, 9:35; Luke 4:43, 8:1, 9:60). It is a message from the God of Abraham, Moses, Jacob, Amos, Hosea, Isaiah: the God who was in Christ. Such a message will never be a mere statement of fact. It will always demand a response.

The question raised by the universal dimensions of the Christian message, therefore, is the consequence of the freedom God gives to humanity. One thing becomes very clear as Christian disciples extend the invitation to belong to the coming reign of God: that for reasons which can by no means be wholly ascribed to the shortcomings of the messenger, the invitation is ignored, snubbed, rejected, and often violently opposed. When we ask what Jesus had to say about this sort of reaction from the world, we find his words to be very harsh; and since they carry the authority of one who was himself despised and rejected, they cannot be ignored.

A Clear Choice

The invitation to salvation is no mere formality. The scriptures make clear that response to the gospel counts for a very great deal. There are alternatives. And in light of the radical claims of the gospel, which we have just reviewed, to say nothing of the candor we have established as the criterion of this study, they are very pressing claims indeed for those of us who wish to take our discipleship seriously. If we are to invite the world to enter into the coming reign of God with candor, the new age of universal *shalom,* then we must be equally candid about what it means to decline the invitation.

THE CRITICAL JUDGMENT OF CHRIST

God's "Krisis"

The New Testament word that best expresses the critical challenge posed by the ministry of Jesus Christ is *krisis,* or judgment. It carries with it the proactive sense of God's justice, the divine initiative of righteousness which requires a human response. Given the human condition of sin, the *krisis* of God is that we must repent, be forgiven, and turn back to God: a conversion *(metanoia)* which is nothing less than a new birth (John 3:16). What makes this *krisis* of God unavoidable is that it is present in Christ, in our midst, and will culminate in a Day of Judgment when all will be judged, "those who have done good, to the resurrection of life, and those who have done evil, to the resurrection of judgment" (John 5:28-29).

Over against the parables describing the growth of the reign of God—the seed and the leaven (Matt. 13:31ff.; Luke 13:20f.)—this critical imagery makes clear that God's coming *shalom* is not only an organic process. It is also a radical healing of a sickness, to which the patient must consent and in which the patient must participate. Thus the Kingdom must be received like a little child (Mark 10:15; Luke 18:17); it must be sought (Mark 15:43); it has standards of behavior which must be observed (Matt. 25:34; I Cor. 6:9f.); and it requires decisive commitment (Luke 9:62). Those who refuse to accept it or its ways will find themselves shut out (Matt. 22:14, 25:12, 30, 46; Gal. 5:21). Moreover, if those who are already part of it fail to honor its conditions, they too will be cast out (Matt. 21:43).

This *krisis* of God uncovers the deeds of those who hitherto have been able to conceal their evil in darkness. Indeed, this is the reality of God's judgment: That light has come into the world in Christ, and exposed these evildoers. Those who receive Christ, and believe in him, are saved. Those who continue in the darkness are condemned (John 3:18-21). God's judgment, therefore, implies a division between those who choose the light of eternal life, and those who remain in the darkness of eternal death (John 5:24). The time to repent, for those who wish to flee from the wrath of God's judgment, is now (Matt. 3:7-10; Mark 1:14-16; John 12:31, 16:11). For those who do not repent, there is divine retribution, and eternal death. Jesus is quite specific: The fires of hell await (Matt. 5:22ff., 7:19). So if anything at all is an impediment in this regard, it must be ruthlessly cut away (Matt. 5:29). There can be no sitting on the fence. Whoever is not for Jesus is by definition against him. Whoever does not work with Jesus, by default destroys his work (Matt. 12:30-32).

Personal merit counts for nothing in this judgment. Even if we were model servants—which of course we are not—we would only be fulfilling our basic job description (Luke 17:7-10). The reality is that we are unworthy servants, for whom dire punishment awaits on the Lord's return (Matt. 21:33-41). Moreover, as we examine the criteria of these parables of return, we must conclude that none of us has a leg on which to stand (Matt. 24:45-51, 25:31-46). The seriousness of the warnings cannot be evaded. We are all to be judged.

Present and Future Judgment

A detailed examination of the apocalyptic material dealing with this future judgment is beyond the scope of this study. Suffice it to say that we should certainly avoid the mistaken use of these texts to try to determine how and when and against whom God's judgment will be meted out.[1] Quite apart from the questionable motives of such enquiries, there is always the tendency to forget that many of the apocalyptic writings were forged in times of persecution. To become engrossed with them in times of relative safety and freedom, therefore, is usually a procrastination over present obligations—a fascination with the future as a means of avoiding what needs to be done here and now. And this the faithful disciple must steadfastly resist.

The real reason why we cannot overlook the seriousness of scriptural teachings on divine judgment, retribution, and eternal life and death, is the same reason it is so powerfully present in the Old

Testament: namely, the unanswered questions of the present. If there are any doubts in this regard, the history of the twentieth century must surely put them to rest. For in our time, the suffering, the genocide, the warfare, and the potential for self-destruction of the human race, have all reached proportions that render the traditional images of hell almost tame by comparison. In the closing months of the Nazi Holocaust, young children were not even gassed before being thrown into the ovens.[2] Whatever the fires of hell might portend, children such as these have had a horrendous foretaste.

Rather than consign these questions of theodicy to the revelations of eternity, therefore, to avoid giving ourselves eschatological headaches, the question which presses is quite the opposite. If so much can happen to children, women, and men in this life, to say nothing of the ecological fabric of the planet, then what might happen in the next life should concern us very much indeed. All that Jesus told us about God's parental care notwithstanding, these holocausts are a matter of record in human history. They have actually taken place. Could it be that an Auschwitz, or something even worse, has a place also in eternity?

With few exceptions, these questions are given scant treatment today, by theologians and pastors alike. For one thing, the issues have been devalued by numerous charlatans, who use them for unscrupulous emotional manipulation. For another, they confront the primary focus of contemporary congregational life, which, as we have already noted, tends to focus on the existential questions of present personhood. But many responsible church leaders avoid them for the altogether legitimate reason that questions of heaven and hell have a very mixed track record in the history of the church, tending to become entangled with the folk religions, which are as endemic to North American culture as anywhere else in the world. Rather than get into such areas of metaphysical discomfort, therefore, many pastoral leaders suggest to enquiring parishioners that things beyond present human experience, such as eternal punishment and reprobation, should be left in the trustworthy hands of a trustworthy God, to be revealed in whatever lies beyond the grave.

The Resurrection of Jesus

This dereliction of theological and pastoral duty—and it is nothing less—stems from a profound mistraditioning of another doctrine, which happens to be the central proclamation of the church: the resurrection of Jesus. Because this too is beyond our present human experience, there are many places in the church where its doctrinal power as historical event has been reduced to subjective faith experience. Originating with the first disciples, and proceeding thence to the heightened life experiences of modern-day Christians, resurrection is often preached today as a spiritual or emotional revitalization. The life-cycle of butterflies and rainbows are symbolically used to affirm that, because the world is alive in the burst of yet another spring, we too can share this latest gift of life from God. We too can be raised with Christ.

So far does this view of the resurrection focus on the immediacy of present life experiences that it tends to overlook the one sure thing about human existence: One day we are all going to die. Our bodies of flesh and blood are going to decay. And never mind how meaningfully we symbolize the cycle of life, or how eloquently we mythologize the hereafter, the deepest questions remain. What happens when I die? What has happened to loved ones who have died? Will there be answers for the pains, the oppressions, the disparities, in short, all that is patently wrong with this world? And in moments of serious self-examination, to what extent will we have to answer for our own shortcomings and wrongdoings before a God who knows us infinitely better than we know ourselves?

Life After Death

Although the resurrection of Jesus leaves most of these questions in the mystery of eternity, where of course they must ultimately remain for the time being, it does give us one central assurance: that there is life after death. Because Jesus was raised from the dead, we can trust his promises of an eternity which is in the hands of a God whose overwhelming concern is our forgiveness and reconciliation. The doctrinal power of the resurrection, therefore, is that it *happened*. There were butterflies before Jesus of Nazareth; there have been butterflies since; but it was Jesus of Nazareth who was raised from the dead when Pontius Pilate was governor of Judea. It is God's definitive word that death is not the final victor. It is the breaking in of eternity into human history, and with it the promise that God's justice and righteousness will prevail.

Paul put it best of all: If Jesus was not raised from the dead, then of all people, Christians are most to be pitied; because they have, or should have, sacrificed much in this world for the hope of that which is to come (I Cor. 15:19). Without the resurrection of Jesus, the only hope we have is that God will judge us with mercy. With his resurrection, we know that the judge is Jesus, who is also our Savior. Without the resurrection of Jesus, the best we can hope for is that one day our children's children will inherit the reign of God. But with his resurrection, we have the much more abundant hope that we will inherit this *basileia* with them. Without the resurrection of Jesus, the children of Auschwitz and Bangladesh and Ethiopia are lost in the depths of God's creative mystery, albeit loving depths. With his resurrection, we know they too will be raised to the life and joy and freedom and food they were deprived of in this life. God's justice and righteousness will settle for nothing less.

Good News for the Poor

One of the ironies of the gospel is that poor and humble folk have never found this message of hope difficult to accept. The objections have come for the most part from those whose earthly comforts have given them the time and the freedom to dwell on such matters. And since there were such people, even in the earliest days of the church, the resurrection has always been the intellectual offense of the gospel, the core of the tradition which has required most traditioning (I Cor. 15:12). The life and death of this Jew from Nazareth were at least verifiable. Whatever the origins of the respective traditions of Jesus, Pilate had ordered his execution.[3] It was another thing, however, to proclaim that he was raised from the dead. This perforce placed the weight of veracity on the witnesses to whom he had appeared, rendering the historicity of the event as much a question as its meaning. We have no record of the actual happening. The scriptural accounts are of Christ's post-resurrection appearances, not the resurrection itself.

Yet the accounts impart more, much more, than a subjective experience of the disciples. The language of the narratives is that of sight and hearing (Matt. 28:9f.; Mark 16:9ff.; Luke 24:13ff., 36ff., 44ff.; John 20:11ff.; Acts 9:3ff.). Christ spoke to those to whom he appeared, or else he would not have been recognized as the one who was crucified. Moreover, the resurrection did not take place as the disciples had been expecting it. The contemporary apocalyptic belief was in a general resurrection, which would herald the end of time, and clearly this did not come to pass.[4] This is why we find Paul making no attempt to argue the point. He proclaimed it as the gospel of Christ, and left it to the Holy Spirit to bear witness to the truth of the matter (I Cor. 2:13).

Unfortunately, there is a long inventory of theories that tries to explain in temporal and often anachronistic terms what was essentially a spiritual happening. At worst, such theories reduce the event to religious superstition, and these need not detain us here. But in more responsible scholarship, and in particular that of the historical-critical method, there are interpretations of the resurrection which attempt to place it in its Judaic setting, yet give it every possible connotation except what the early church said it was—something that happened to Jesus, not to the disciples. Such attempts usually begin with philosophical presuppositions which, as Richard R. Niebuhr perceptively observed, hold the content of the early church's faith to be normative, but mistrust its mental processes.[5]

Gospel and Theology

The fundamental confusion is the same one we shall soon identify at the heart of our dilemma over discipleship—the failure to distinguish between the gospel tradition and its theological significance. We accept the tradition in faith; we affirm it, and we proclaim it. We also reflect on it theologically. But we must not confuse these tasks. For when theological reflection takes the place of the tradition, the gospel is disempowered, and we break faith with the faithful.[6] If our task as Christian disciples is to proclaim the gospel as we have it in scripture, then we cannot consign its scandalous particularities to the category of divine mystery simply as a theological or pastoral expedient.

What Paul handed over to the Gentiles, and what has been handed on to us across the centuries, is the message we too must proclaim to the world in which we live:

> that Christ died for our sins in accordance with the scriptures, that he was buried, that he was raised on the third day in accordance with the scriptures, and that he appeared to Cephas, then to the twelve. Then he appeared to more than five hundred brethren at one time, most of whom are still alive, though some have fallen asleep. Then he appeared to James, then to all the apostles. Last of all, as to one untimely born, he appeared also to me. (I Cor. 15:3-8)

Guaranteed Salvation

One theologian who has done much to restore the doctrinal significance of the resurrection to contemporary Christology is Jürgen Moltmann, whose *Theology of Hope* has been a watershed in setting the eschatological agenda of the church for our time. He describes the Bultmannian interpretation of the resurrection as shifting "the 'reality' of the resurrection from something that happens to the crucified Jesus to something that happens to the existence of the disciples," thereby making Christology the variable and anthropology the constant.[7] By contrast, Moltmann views the resurrection as the eschatological promise of a God who was already known for keeping promises and giving new hope. The raising of Jesus from the dead was thus the ultimate warrant of God's saving-righteousness:

> The divine word in Christ is new solely because its fulfillment can no longer be endangered or abolished, as once was the case, but has become incontestable; and it is unique, despite all its varied earthly movement and manifold testimony and despite its prolepsis in the Old Testament because in Christ it not only reveals anew the one eschatological salvation, but in addition also conclusively *guarantees* the realizing of that salvation.[8]

Guaranteed Judgment

This is the doctrinal substance of the resurrection of Jesus that makes it so central to the gospel of the coming reign of God. But the immediate and sobering corollary, of course, is that God's judgment also is conclusively guaranteed, when all things will be revealed, and the secrets of all hearts will be judged (Matt. 10:26; Rom. 2:16). The question therefore becomes how such a radical judgment, with all of the threats—and threats they are—of punishment for those who fail to repent, of eternal perdition and eternal death, can be compatible with the universal hope pervading the whole of scripture.

One approach to this apparent contradiction we must immediately discount, namely the collation of biblical texts to see which is the more important theme. This is exegetically inappropriate, since it disdains the editors of scripture, whose work is a vital part of Christian tradition. The church affirms the spiritual inspiration of these compilers in determining the authoritative witness of the Bible no less than that of those who did the writing. We must therefore accept that they included such dire warnings for a purpose. The consequences of turning away from God cannot be overlooked. They are in the scriptures; and these writings are the book of the church.[9]

Selective Redemption

Another approach we must also reject is a selective view of God's salvation. There are many variations to this, but they have one thing in common: the belief that not everyone is going to be saved. Whether this stems from a doctrine of double predestination, according to which God consigns some persons to salvation and others to perdition, or from a radical doctrine of free will, according to which God allows all of us to determine our own future, this belief ultimately rests on the interpretation of scripture that only through a personal trust in Jesus Christ as Savior can anyone inherit eternal life. Accordingly, the fact that many people refuse to accept the atoning work of Christ in their lives means that many are not going to spend eternity in heaven. The whole purpose of being a Christian, therefore, is to ensure a place in eternity as opposed to those who will not have one.

We need to be clear at this point that we are not talking about those religious elitists whose emotional and spiritual insecurities lead them to assert their identity at the expense of everyone else. Leon Festinger and others have long since exposed the social neuroses of such a stance.[10] Nor yet are we talking about the tricksters, whose offers of eternal benefits are periodically reinforced with warnings of what will happen if they are ignored. The yearnings of such persons for mansions in the sky would be more credible if they did not give quite so much attention to the mansions they accumulate here on earth. We are talking rather of those who genuinely seek to share the gospel with as many as they can, and as often as they can, in the sincere hope that everyone will repent and accept the salvation offered in Jesus Christ, but who are equally convinced that eternal punishment and perdition await those who decline.

Universalist Polarities

It is this conviction which, more than any other, polarizes the North American church today. It puzzles and angers many from the liberal traditions, who cannot understand why the prospect of eternal punishment should figure so prominently in a gospel of love. The puzzlement and anger are no less vigorous on the part of many evangelical Christians, who feel that disdain for eternal punishment renders evangelism a pointless exercise, and worse, devalues the atonement of Jesus Christ. "Universalism" has thus become a very polemical word, and particularly for a great many conservative Christians. In one sense, their attitude is understandable, for these are the persons whose approach to evangelism involves them in some very direct interpersonal sharing of the gospel, and who therefore encounter the daunting enigma of persistent rejection, something many of us manage to avoid by never risking it in the first place. Thus the parables of separation at the end of time, such as the wheat and the tares (Matt. 13:24-30), speak powerfully to their experiences in evangelistic outreach. The gnashing of teeth in the furnace of fire will be an unspeakable tragedy (Matt. 13:40-43); but what else can be determined about the fate of persons whose stubborn rejection of the grace of Christ has been a reckless tempting of God?

Yet this too we must reject as an ultimately parochial view of God's salvation. It is not rejected lightly, because the earnestness with which it is held is directly proportional to the evangelistic energy and outreach of those who hold it. They give more of their time, risk more of their dignity, and expend more of their emotional and spiritual resources on such work than their less conservative Christian colleagues ever acknowledge. Even so, if we are to wrestle with the tension of our discipleship in the deepest sense of the word, we must seek an approach that, while taking fully into account the rigor of God's justice, focuses on the central truth of scripture: that God's supreme nature is one of saving-righteousness; and that divine justice is supremely declared in God's covenant to save the whole of God's creation.

God's Biased Justice

There are a number of reasons for taking this approach. All of them have been implicit in our argument thus far, but it is time now to make them explicit. First, the justice of God is not impartial. Not only is it biased toward the poor and the helpless, but also it is weighted toward mercy. This much was clear in the Old Testament prophets, but in Christ it is fully revealed. God's purpose in Christ is not to condemn, but to save the world. This servant of God will not break the bruised reed, or quench the dimly burning wick; nor will God falter or be discouraged until this justice is brought to victory and established in the earth (Isa. 42:1-4; Matt. 12:18-21).

If God's justice were indeed an impartial system, with God as impartial judge, then we truly would be without hope. But God has taken an initiative, unilateral and unequivocal, to declare that all of us are welcome back home where we belong. This is the whole weight of Jesus' ministry, and it is a cardinal misunderstanding of God if we apply the criteria of impartial judgment to a judge who has declared a very partial agenda indeed.

God's Parental Suffering

Another reason for taking a universal approach is the mystery of evil and suffering in the world, otherwise known as the questions of theodicy. Irrespective of the gospel, countless millions of human beings have lived, and continue to live, nasty, brutish lives, brought to ghastly culmination in the various holocausts of this century. This reality tests the parental oversight of God, and our dependent relationship, as never before. The title character in William Styron's novel, *Sophie's Choice*, speaks for voiceless millions as she is shipped to a concentration camp:

> But as Auschwitz loomed more and more inevitably and now, on the train, made itself inescapable, Sophie was smothered by the realization that she was victim of punishment by association, retribution through chance concurrence. She kept saying to herself: I don't belong here. . . .
> But among other ironies, she realized, was this one: she had not been *judged* guilty of anything, merely interrogated and forgotten. She had then been thrown in haphazardly among these partisans, where she was victim less of any specific retributive justice than of a general rage—a kind of berserk lust for complete domination and oppression.[11]

If so much evil can be visited on so many innocent people, and especially innocent children, then the justice of God cannot be an impartial, objective legal system. If it is, then it is a system in which the errors are monumental; and God, in the role of impartial judge, has a very great deal to explain. Moreover, even if we complement this role with that of heavenly Father, as Jesus taught us to do, there are still judicial questions to be answered. Human parents in North America who allow even one child to die from lack of food are jailed on grounds of child neglect. What verdict, then, would we pronounce on the heavenly parent, who has permitted, and continues to permit, millions of children to die from neglect?[12]

God's Saving-Righteousness

The only possible way out of this legal "Catch-22" is to remember that this is not how God's justice works; that God is a God of *saving*-righteousness, not forensic judgment. Which is why the argument that Christ's death, the death of an innocent, was necessary in order to satisfy the demands of an absolute justice is profoundly to misunderstand justice in the Old Testament sense of the word. Although there is a deep sense in which Jesus takes our place on the cross, and dies on our behalf, this cannot be regarded as a legal substitution. That is to disregard the saving quality of God's righteousness (*ṣedeq*), and turn the incarnation of Jesus Christ inside out.[13] Instead of Jesus becoming human to save us from our sin, it portrays Jesus as a forensic mechanism, whose chief purpose is to satisfy a wrathful God—a God whose omniscience and omnipotence apparently could not divine an alternative to what was patently a failed experiment. This theory of the atonement perhaps had a place in a world where honor was held in high esteem, and where dishonor was a state worse than death.[14] But to hold to it in the late twentieth century in North America is judicial technics gone mad. It is to impose onto the divine nature the most grotesque dimensions of the human psyche. It is the anthropomorphic rape of God.

God's Saving Time

The most compelling reason for taking a universal approach to God's salvation, however, is that the warnings of God's judgment must be placed against the backdrop of human history. To understand the significance of this, we must return to the distinction Geoffrey Wainwright has drawn between the "horizontal" and "vertical" dimensions of eschatology.[15] In the New Testament, this distinction is found in the use of the Greek words *chronos*, meaning duration or measurable time, long or short (Matt. 25:19; Luke 4:5), and *kairos*, meaning a point of time, a decisive moment of opportunity or fulfillment, or time with a particular content (Matt. 13:30; Mark 1:15; Luke 8:13).

In the Old Testament, this distinction is not made very clearly, because the concept of time which emerges overwhelmingly from the Hebrew bible is that all moments, seasons, and the whole of history—past, present, and future—are in God's hands (Exod. 33:5; Deut. 11:12; Ps. 31:15, 90:4; Isa. 60:19-20). Although there is a sense of progression, in which God delivers the people of Israel from captivity (Lev. 11:45; Num. 15:41) and brings them to the promised land (Deut. 11:8-12; Josh. 21:43-45), the ultimate hope of the Hebrews is the "day of the Lord," the omnipresence of God's righteousness, when "the Lord alone will be exalted" (Isa. 2:12-18; Jer. 31:31-34).

It is highly significant, therefore, that in the New Testament, *kairos* appears far more often than *chronos*, and is used in the sense of something new and unprecedented which takes the place of what has gone before. This *kairos* of Christ is a "breaking in" of God's time of justice, calling humankind to repentance, forgiveness, reconciliation, and righteousness. Jesus brings a new teaching (Mark 1:27), a new commandment (John 13:34; I John 2:7ff.), new cloth, new wine, and new treasure (Mark 2:21-22; Matt. 13:52). But most important of all, he brings the dawning of a new age, a new *aion*, in which all things and all persons will be made new (Isa. 43:19; II Cor. 5:17; Gal. 6:15; Eph. 2:15). This new age will come to fulfillment with the *parousia* of Jesus Christ, until which time Christian disciples are charged with announcing it and manifesting its firstfruits in a community of active expectancy, the *ekklēsia*.

The important thing to remember about all of these aspects of time —the *chronos* of historical progression, the *kairos* of critical moment, and the *aion* of eternal hope—is that they all belong to God. They are God's time, to be dispensed as God wills, and to be brought to fulfillment as God chooses. This means that the nature of God as we have discerned it thus far—God's saving-righteousness, God's justice, and God's love—permeates the whole of time. The chronology of humanity is a history of God's saving-righteousness (*sedeq*), and also of God's justice (*krisis*). The decisive moment of time also belongs to God, the *kairos* of prophetic pronouncement, critical choice, and unprecedented opportunity. And the new age (*aion*) which will replace this world order is also of God, when justice will no longer have to pronounce against sin and evil and suffering, because righteousness will prevail, on earth as in heaven.

These concepts can further explain for us the tensions the delayed *parousia* imposed on the early church. It was one thing to look for "the day of the Lord," with open anticipation for that which was to come. It was altogether another thing to declare that this "day" had come in the person of Jesus Christ, and then be confronted with a shortfall in the promises hitherto associated with it. The progression of *chronos* time was therefore an increasing factor in the self-understanding of the Christian community, as the church forged the dogmas of the tradition and at the same time endeavored to sustain its faith stance of active expectancy. Theologically, these tensions were drawn together into a doctrine which, though it never became a credal statement, reflected the integrity of the early church in its twofold task of traditioning— handling over the *kairos* of the gospel to the world, and handing it on chronologically to the next generation of Christian disciples. It is the doctrine of *recapitulation.*

Recapitulation

The idea of recapitulation is drawn from two New Testament words: *apokatástasis,* the restoration, or restitution of the human race to its former state (Acts 3:21); and *anakephalaíōsis,* the re-uniting, or regathering of all things under the headship of Christ (Eph. 1:10, 22). As a doctrine, it was first given definitive expression in the writings of the second-century bishop of Lyons, Irenaeus, who drew heavily from the Pauline passages that deal with the role of Christ in establishing a new humanity.[16] Irenaeus identifies the whole human race with Adam, the one who failed to realize his potential and became disobedient to God. Thus Adam's fall was not something which subsequently affected human history, but was in fact the fall of humankind as a whole. Adam and the human race are mystically one and the same. By the same token, Jesus Christ and the human race are one and the same. Jesus is the new human being, and what the human race lost in Adam is recovered in Jesus Christ. The key to this work of Christ is his obedience, even unto death. It is not his incarnation *per se* that brings about the redemption of humanity, but the way in which he lived and died. Those who are in Christ, therefore, are to live in the same way, as befits a race which has been given a new start.

The inclusiveness and universality of these concepts are taken even further by the third-century exponent of the doctrine, Origen, who was head of the catechetical school in Alexandria. With what has been described as an "ontological idealism," Origen extended the doctrine to include not only the world, but also everything that emanates from God.[17] Drawing on I Corinthians 15:25-28, he equates the beginning of all things with the end. The final consummation of Christ's salvation will thus be the reconciliation with God of the whole of creation, including death, and even including Satan. Nothing at all will be lost.[18]

Christ's Long, Slow Victory

This teaching has branded Origen for many as an unsound universalist, albeit owing to an "optimism of grace."[19] However, as Benjamin Drewery's study of his doctrine of grace makes clear, Origen's universalism is solidly grounded in a profoundly scriptural eschatology, in which the first advent of Christ is intelligible only in light of the second.[20] The issue is not soteriological selection (the salvation of some as opposed to others), but eschatological fulfillment (the ultimate salvation of all).

This brings two seemingly contradictory truths into a deeply moving unity. On the one hand, we have the clear scriptural declaration that Christ died for the whole of humanity, affording salvation for all. On the other hand, we have the equally clear declaration that this salvation is only for those who believe in Christ. Without compromising either of these truths, Origen places them in their proper perspective—the majestic sweep of God's eternity. It is through Christ and Christ alone that we are saved; but the fullness of God's salvation is that one day the whole of creation, everyone and everything, will accept this gracious gift and share in it—the long, slow victory of Christ over all the enemies of humankind, the last of which is death. The cross thus initiates the birth and growth of an ultimately worldwide Christian community, culminating in the final universal reconciliation to God of all things.[21]

Here we have, in a synthesis of *kairos, chronos,* and *aion,* at least a handle by which to grasp the deep tension between Jesus' promises of eternal life and warnings of eternal punishment. There is a cosmic struggle taking place for the salvation of planet Earth, consisting of countless confrontations between Jesus Christ and the forces of evil. As it concerns us, the struggle is for one wayward child at a time, in which the Holy Spirit will invite and plead, and in which Christ will ultimately confront from the cross. As it concerns the cosmos, the struggle is against "principalities, against the powers, against the world rulers of this present darkness, against the spiritual hosts of wickedness in the heavenly places" (Eph. 6:12). The *krisis* of God's justice, whether personal or cosmic, will always pose the dire consequences of turning away from God. Such penalties are not, and never will be, empty threats. But by the same token, the scope of Christ's triumph will never be reduced to the outcome of particular skirmishes. The long, slow victory of Christ will be won, all temporary setbacks notwithstanding. The words of Robert Frost express this very well:

> Things must expect to come in front of us
> A many times—I don't say just how many—
> That varies with the things—before we see them.
> One of the lies would make it out that nothing
> Ever presents itself before us twice.
> Where would we be at last if that were so?
> Our very life depends on everything's
> Recurring till we answer from within.
> The thousandth time may prove the charm.[22]

Eternal Grace and Judgment

Our problem, as we shall see in the next chapter, is that we have greatly exaggerated our own importance in this cosmic drama. We have focused on our particular faith response to Jesus Christ to the neglect of the larger issues involved. As a result, our understanding of biblical time is seriously warped. We take the "vertical" dimension of God's eschatological hope, the *kairos* of Christ's call to repentance and forgiveness, and confuse it with the "horizontal" dimension, the *chronos* of human history. Were this not so detrimental to the gospel, it would be laughable as the most clumsy of soteriological bad manners. It is an attempt to restrict the grace of Jesus Christ, the risen Christ, who is universally present in the power of the Holy Spirit and heir to the coming reign of God, to our present understandings of human existence. It is to dare to imply that God's grace is limited to this side of the grave. The enormity of the error is matched only by its pomposity.

In the pastoral ministry of the church, however, the results have been, and continue to be, nothing less than tragic. Countless Christians have mourned the death of loved ones with a cruel and unnecessary burden. Because they did not "make a decision for Christ," or "ask Jesus Christ to be their Savior," or "give their lives to Christ" before they died, these persons have been consigned to the terrible unknowns of eternal punishment, which their surviving relatives and friends have experienced vicariously with deep emotional anguish. Whereas biblical time in all its dimensions makes clear that God's grace is by no means limited to this side of the grave. The scriptures are appropriately cautious about details, but the psalmist is in no doubt at all about the reality: "If I ascend to heaven, thou art there! / If I make my bed in Sheol, thou art there!" (Ps. 139:8). Paul is equally sure that "neither death, nor life, nor angels, nor principalities, nor things present, nor things to come, nor powers, nor height, nor depth, nor anything else in all creation, will be able to separate us from the love of God in Christ Jesus our Lord" (Rom. 8:38-39).

Quite apart from scriptural referents, however, it stands to reason that God does not foreclose on sinners in this life. There is first the obvious historical fact that we have almost completed two millennia of Christian history, and billions of human beings have been born and have died without hearing the gospel. Moreover, the eschatological clock is still running, and people are still being born and are still dying without hearing the gospel. There are those who remonstrate that this is due to Christian lethargy, and who are mounting monumental efforts to put it right, motivated in some instances by the impulse to fulfill the prophecy that "this gospel of the kingdom will be preached throughout the whole world, as a testimony to all nations; and then the end will come" (Matt. 24:14).[23]

Two factors, however, make this a highly tenuous stance. First, even if the gospel were to be universally preached, it begs the question of how often the good news of salvation has been, and continues to be, discredited by Christians who make mistakes, or worse, dishonor their calling. Once again, it becomes impossible to apply criteria of impartial justice. For if persons are to be tried in an eternal court for neglecting to respond to the gospel as it is regularly proclaimed and demonstrated by the average North American congregation, any competent defense lawyer would immediately, and successfully, appeal. Which is, of course, precisely what Christ does for us in eternity:

He ever lives above
  For me to intercede;
  His all-redeeming love,
    His precious blood to plead.
His blood atoned for all our race,
And sprinkles now the throne of grace.
                · · · · ·
The Father hears him pray,
  His dear anointed One;
He cannot turn away
  The presence of his Son:
His Spirit answers to the blood,
And tells me I am born of God.

My God is reconciled,
  His pard'ning voice I hear;
He owns me for his child,
  I can no longer fear:
With confidence I now draw nigh,
And, Father, Abba, Father, cry![24]

The second reason why response to the gospel in this life cannot be viewed as the soteriological determinant of grace is that God's judgment has no such perimeters either. The scriptural injunctions are clear: God is no respecter of persons (Rom. 2:11; II Cor. 5:10). God's *krisis* will continue into all eternity along with God's *agapē*. To limit either of these divine characteristics to this life only is once again to restrict God to anthropomorphic concepts of time. Neither God's judgment nor God's righteousness is limited to this age: They are eternal, as is God. There will always be God's judgment, and there will always be God's grace.

This is why the most severe warnings from Jesus are directed, not against those who are ignorant of God, but against those who know God and refuse to obey God's law (Matt. 21:28-32, 33-41; 23:23-36; 25:24-30, 41-46). It is also why Jesus cautioned against judging others, in any way whatsoever (Matt. 7:1f.; Rom. 14:4). For as all things are brought under Christ, not only are we ruled by God's *ṣedeq-sedaqah*, but also God's searching *krisis* probes every nook and cranny of unrighteousness, including residual resistance in the Christian. We go on, not only from grace to grace, but also from repentance to repentance.

An Analogy

It might be helpful in this regard to return to the analogy of the American Revolution.[25] Some two hundred years ago, events took place which radically altered the history and the identity of the North American continent. Instead of continuing as subjects of King George III of England, the inhabitants of thirteen colonies declared themselves citizens of the United States of America. The result is that today, anyone who is born in the United States is an American citizen. That is enacted the day they are born, and without so much as by their leave. They may ultimately choose to relinquish their privileges. But unless and until they do so, their citizenship is a birthright. Their choice is not whether to accept it, but whether or not they wish to keep it. And, as we know, the great majority do not even think of exercising that option at all.

The analogy has further ramifications. To begin with, not everyone was in favor of the revolution when it took place. Most people sat on the fence, waiting to see whether George Washington would emerge as a national hero, or a British traitor. Then there is the fact that the revolution by no means covered the continent at first. There were those in the Mississippi Valley who remained French in their political alignments, just as there were those in the Southwest who remained Spanish. For that matter, there were those in Appalachia who probably didn't know about the revolution for half a century or more.

Then again, the ideals of the revolution were by no means immediately fulfilled; many remain unfulfilled. If one was a woman at the time of the Revolutionary War, it was arguable how much independence had in fact been won. If one was black, it was arguable not at all. If one was a native American, the Declaration of Independence was not only moot; it was also a dire warning of the working out of a destiny which, to the current occupants of the land, not to mention those of the remainder of the hemisphere, was by no means manifest.

The Birthright of Salvation

Like all analogies, this one breaks down at points; and most certainly the purpose is not to suggest parallels between God's salvation and American covenant history.[26] But there are important inferences we can draw with regard to our soteriological inheritance. First, it is vitally important to place the weight of our salvation on what Christ did for us two thousand years ago, without our permission. In Christ, the human race was declared salvageable, and its controlling powers wrested from Beelzebul, the prince of darkness. There is much yet to be done to bring this to fulfillment. Many members of the human race, still suffering under the old regime, have yet to benefit from what happened; many are still sitting on the fence; and many do not yet know what has happened. But every human being born on planet Earth inherits that salvation as a birthright. The question is not whether or not to accept it, but whether or not to reject it.

At this juncture, there are those who will ask what is the purpose of evangelism, or even the point of being a Christian. If Christ has accomplished our salvation, is the proclamation of the Good News at all efficacious? Is there any point in committing to a costly discipleship in order to take this Good News to the ends of the earth? Is human response to the gospel of any significance, if our salvation is in fact a birthright by virtue of our very humanity?

The answer is a resounding Yes! to each of these questions. For the quantum difference between the coming reign of God and the development of the United States, or any other country for that matter, is that the ruler of the kingdom of God has been named. Moreover, having been named, and having won the pivotal battle against the forces of evil in the world, this Ruler is now primarily concerned with putting right what is wrong, healing what is diseased, and restoring planet Earth to its rightful place in the cosmos. Accordingly, no citizen of this planet can merely inherit this birthright. The birthright must be realized in a way of life which is compatible with the coming reign of God. The children of God must behave like children of God. Then, and only then, will Christ's work be done.

The Point of Evangelism and Discipleship

The reason and the purpose for evangelism, and for being a Christian disciple, is to help Jesus with this unfinished task. As long as there is pain or suffering in the world; as long as there is injustice or oppression; as long as any of Christ's little ones hurt, or starve, or are neglected, Jesus suffers with them (Matt. 25:42-45). What more pressing motivation could there be for a Christian to evangelize than to bring Christ's suffering to an end, as quickly and as thoroughly as possible?

The Good News is that Jesus has inaugurated a new age when love and peace and justice will prevail. Christian disciples must ensure that this word gets out, and that it reaches those who can do something about it. For as long as the secular powers of the world are indifferent to God's justice, Jesus is snubbed and dishonored as the legitimate ruler of this planet. Beelzebul has been dethroned, and there is no longer any need to bow at that altar. Powerful persons need to hear that word; and even if at first it seems to be bad news rather than good, they will ultimately be grateful for its radical liberation.[27]

Carl Braaten, whose work in clarifying the uniqueness and universality of the gospel has been seminal for contemporary theology, addresses the issue from a profoundly Christocentric perspective:

> The good news is that all people have been united with God in Christ. One chief difference between the Christian and the non-Christian is that the one knows and the other does not yet know. That difference, of course, makes a lot of difference. The point, however, is that the Christ-event is full; there is no void which has to be filled up by the church or the world. The evangelistic task of the church is to bear witness to the word and deed of God in Jesus Christ. Christ alone is the true minister, the true missionary of God *par excellence*. All of us are more like acolytes assisting in the priestly and prophetic ministry of Christ.[28]

Welcome Home!

It is this which, when all has been said and done, is the best news of all: that Christ is our prophet and priest, our judge and our hope. In Christ we have the assurance that God wants all people to be part of the heavenly family, taking full advantage of their new birthright. This is the work of grace that transcends the heights and plumbs the depths of our being as we never thought possible. Not only are we forgiven all that separates us from God, past, present, or future, and whether or not we are to blame. We are reconciled to God in a new relationship, which can best be described in two words: Welcome Home! It was the purpose of Jesus' ministry to make this possible for everyone. Indeed, Jesus is the missing person in his own parable of the prodigal son (Luke 15:11-32). The son came to understand how headstrong and foolish he had been, and the father wanted him back with all the yearnings he had felt when he released him to waste his inheritance.

But Jesus himself gave the parable new meaning, by coming in person to invite us back home, and by giving his life to bring all prodigals to their senses. He extended this invitation supremely from the cross, making clear how serious was the human predicament, and how lethal. No self-justification, no excuse, no rationalization could ever again disguise the awful reality of human sin. For those who represented humankind two thousand years ago, it may have been a matter of mistaken identity. For God, it was a matter of life and death.

When we look at the cross, and remember our own spiritual homecoming, we realize how much God was willing to risk, and continues to risk, to have us back home. For God will always give us the freedom to accept this gracious invitation, or refuse it. We can all recall what it is like to be rejected by someone, even by a stranger; and much worse, the shock and the pain of rejection by a friend, a spouse, a daughter, or a son. We can then begin to sense the depth of God's anguish throughout human history. Not one prodigal, but millions of daughters and sons across the centuries have lived their lives away from their true home. Alienated from their true family, they have suffered from the ravages of human sin, either as sinners, or as those who are sinned against. It is incalculable how much grief and torment this has heaped on a God who is more loving and protective than any human mother, more trustworthy and concerned than any earthly father.

This is why our surrender to God's grace, our acceptance of God's invitation to come home, is such an overwhelmingly joyous occasion. On our part, it is the relief of giving up a pointless struggle. Never mind what *we* would like to do with our lives; the reality is that we are God's family, and that's that. But there is more, much more, to our homecoming. It is the welcome we receive even when we are a long way off. It is the joy of the household of heaven that the latest prodigals have returned to claim their birthright. It surpasses anything we could ever have imagined. Wherever our Christian discipleship may lead us thereafter, we will never lose this joy of knowing that we are back where we belong.

Empty Places

And yet, even in our moments of deepest communion with God, our joy remains guarded. We know that our festivities must remain muted, for the homecoming celebration has not yet begun in earnest. There are still empty places at the table. There are sinners who still need to come to their senses. There are millions of God's family still without enough to eat. There are countless little ones of God still being sinned against with all the demonic ingenuity of a prodigal human race. We must help to invite them home. We must help Christ dry their tears and heal their wounds—all of them.

Does this weaken the *krisis* of God's justice, or compromise the *kairos* of Christ's new age? Not at all: The warnings and the judgment are in place for all eternity. What it does say is this: Should there be, at the *parousia* of Jesus Christ, even one of God's family who, after repeated entreaties and boundless parental care and concern, stubbornly refuses to accept his birthright of salvation, and turns away from God for ever and ever; should there be even one such creature, then God's cry of anguish will rend the cosmos, and the heavenly feast will be eaten in a terrible, terrible silence.

SALVATION AND DISCIPLESHIP: A NECESSARY DISTINCTION

The Source of the Blockage

We are close now to the source of our ecclesial blockage. We have gone back to the originative witness of the church in scripture, and seen how the people of God, from the time of Abraham, have been called for a purpose: to declare the universal grace of God. They are heraldic messengers, evangelists, and their message is that God is a God of righteousness and justice, a saving God, whose care and concern is for all the world, but most especially for the helpless and the needy. We have seen how this message of Good News was definitively revealed in Jesus Christ, who came, not to pronounce condemnation on humankind, but with a critical invitation to repent and come home to God's family, an invitation extended supremely from the cross. After his resurrection, he commissioned the new Israel, the church, to announce the *basileia tou theou*, the coming reign of God, and to tell the world to be ready for its fulfillment in a new age of universal love, peace, and justice. Moreover, like God's commission to the Israelites, this message of Good News was to be shared with all nations.

We saw what happens, however, when this universal commission is viewed by the people of God as privilege rather than responsibility. The grace of God then becomes blocked. The people of God, rejecting their covenant, become religiously possessive, and are thereby caught in a self-contradiction. For in their endeavor to concentrate God's grace into their particular covenant relationship, they lose it. God cannot be thus domesticated; nor can God's grace be thus restricted. God will seek other channels and other servants.

97

We noted how Paul confronted the Jerusalem church with these alternatives, and the premise of our study is that the same issue faces us today in the North American church. Will we accept the grace of God as a universal grace? Or will we, albeit with a readiness to share it with others, try to focus it on our own particular faith experiences, and thereby cause it to be blocked?

Like all blockages, this one will finally be cleared, not so much by dislodging the obstacle, as by the sheer force of what is meant to flow through the channel in the first place. The gospel of Jesus Christ in its fullness will reopen our ecclesial arteries—or bypass them. Our priority, therefore, must be to discern the reason for the blockage, so that we might facilitate its clearance and be ready for the grace which will surely then flow through. As we have suggested at various stages in our investigation, to be bypassed and judged as unworthy servants would be a waste of tremendous ecclesial potential.[1] It is also quite unnecessary, if we will only engage in a modicum of contextual self-evaluation.

A Protestant Self-Evaluation

To do this, we shall draw on the work of Robert E. Cushman, and in particular his collected essays, *Faith Seeking Understanding.*[2] The underlying thesis of this volume is that our Protestant theological heritage is rooted in a context of considerable particularity, which by and large we have failed to acknowledge, primarily because of the predominance of Western culture during the past four hundred years. In the fourteenth and fifteenth centuries, argues Cushman, there emerged in Western thought, under Scotist and Occamist influence, a doctrine of absolute divine sovereignty in which there was no intelligible connection between nature and divine grace or between humankind and God. It was this philosophical background against which the Reformation theology of the European continent was formulated and which it reflects: salvation by grace alone through faith alone. Since there is no way at all from humankind to God, scripture alone shows an opened way from God to humankind.[3]

Thus the Reformation doctrine of God and humankind was inherited, not from the New Testament but from a widely influential Occamistic philosophy. The only intelligible relations between the sovereign Creator and the creation, or between God and the human race, were those provided by God's immediate omnipotent will and act, which in turn deprived human nature of any inherent dignity. Along with the dissolution of the inherent structures of the created order of due natural process, this orphaned the human race, leading in the seventeenth century to those philosophical and theological initiatives which gave humankind not only independence from God, but also a newly discovered and insistent subjectivity.[4]

These are broad brushstrokes with which to fill a canvas, but for those of us in the Protestant tradition, the conclusion of Cushman's diagnosis is a self-illumination of some magnitude:

> In the secular world, this [subjectivity] took the form of the self-preoccupation with the ego-self; and in religion, it took the form of what we usually speak of as "modern Protestant theology." And, at this point, Christian faith, in the New Testament sense, was successively translated into some species or other of the human self-consciousness. With Kant, it was the moral-consciousness, or the God-consciousness (Schleiermacher), the value-consciousness (Ritschl), the religious *a priori* (Troeltsch), religious experience (Wm. James), ultimate concern (Tillich) authentic self-understanding (Bultmann).
>
> In each case, the presuppositions have been the same, the isolation of man as the *de facto* starting point for theological understanding. In every case there is implicitly the same problem—the Cartesian problem. It is the question whether and how the human religious potential reaches as far as God, on the one hand, and, on the other, whether this is the same God whose thunders still sound from Sinai, whose Glory is radiated in the face of the Christ of the New Testament as the Word of God. How shall the two be brought together? In a word, that is the problem of modern Protestant theology.[5]

An Anthropocentric Gospel

And, we might add, of our Christian discipleship also. For with this broad historical canvas, Cushman has identified the source of our North American ecclesial blockage: the anthropocentric domestication of God; the enculturation of the gospel *par excellence*. Although we clearly must share some responsibility for this in our own day and age, it nonetheless lifts a considerable burden to realize that it was our Protestant forebears who set the course. As Feuerbach observed as long ago as 1843 in his first two principles of the philosophy of the future:

The task of the modern era was the realization and humanization of God—the transformation and dissolution of theology into anthropology. The religious or practical form of this humanization was Protestantism . . . [which] is no longer concerned, as Catholicism is, about what God is in himself, but about what he is for man. . . . It is no longer theology; it is essentially Christology, that is, religious anthropology.[6]

That there are serious theological differences in how this anthropocentrism is expressed does nothing to diminish it. Indeed, these very differences have served to reinforce it, since Western Protestants, and particularly those of us in North America, have exported our theological agendas to other parts of the world, demanding (usually with cash in hand) that everyone else take sides in what is essentially a longstanding domestic dispute. For the fact of the matter is that the evangelically born-again Christian and the liberal Christian questing for authentic existence are but two horses from the same stable. Both are focused on human questions rather than those of God, and both are more concerned with human response to the gospel than what God has to say about the human condition. Whereas the pressing question for the Christian is how to discern the will of God in an obedient discipleship without succumbing on the one hand to a selective and parochial soteriology, or on the other to a philosophical syncretism; for the one isolates Christian discipleship, and the other enervates it.

If we accept this diagnosis of an anthropocentric blindspot in Protestantism, our self-evaluation today must be clear, and radical. The question is nothing less than whether it is possible to be in communion with God, irrespective of Christian faith. This is not to say irrespective of Christ; for Christ inexorably remains at the center of God's salvation. But it is to ask, in common parlance, whether it is possible to be saved by Christ without being a Christian.

Beyond the Law: Beyond the Church

Paul's answer in his day rings loud and clear in our own: Yes, indeed it is.[7] Just as it was possible then to know God and to become a Christian without the benefit of the Jewish law, so today we must affirm that it is possible to know God, the God who is also Christ and Holy Spirit, without the particular knowledge which comes to those whose privilege and obligation it is to be Christian disciples.

The ground of this affirmation, which is not nearly so radical as our

Western theological anthropocentrism might make it seem, is of course the eschatological hope of the resurrection. As we noted in the last chapter, God's soteriological chronometer is still running. The theological constructs of Paul, based on centuries of Jewish history, must now be extended by two millennia of church history. To the semantics of Jew and Greek must now be added those of Christian and non-Christian. And if Paul was concerned to place Jew and Gentile under the same accountability to the gospel, yet eschatologically without the advantage of the law, so it must be our concern to place Christian and non-Christian under the same accountability to God's saving-righteousness and justice, yet eschatologically without the advantage of the gospel.

It is this soteriological vision our anthropocentrism persistently prevents us from claiming. Thus the flow of God's universal grace is blocked, and we are distracted from an authentic discipleship by salvific concerns which are properly God's agenda, and God's alone.

An Early Protestant Course-Correction

A frequently overlooked chapter in our Protestant heritage is that this potential theological impediment was perceived at an early date by the English Reformers, who looked very cautiously on the developments in continental Protestant theology. There are some who would argue that this is because the English are basically a dull race; that the exciting characters and episodes in British history have come from Scotland or Ireland or Wales, whereas the English tend to take life much as it comes. Whether or not this is the reason, the fact is that English church scholars looked on the continental theologians with a marked degree of circumspection.

The key years in this regard were the 1530s and 1540s, during which time England might well have become a Lutheran country but for the mutual antipathy of Luther and Henry VIII. Since Henry was perhaps the most promising theologian ever to occupy the English throne (the pope named him "Defender of the Faith" for his *Defense of the Seven Sacraments*) it was most unfortunate that Luther should have referred to him as "a wretched scribbler."[8] But their disagreement meant that the English church was under royal directive to take a *via media*, giving English Protestantism a very different compass heading. The breach between Henry and Rome was largely political, an interesting indication of which is that modern British coinage still designates the reigning monarch defender of the faith!

Perhaps the clearest theological statement of those years is to be found in the *Homilies* of the Church of England. They are at once a rich taproot of the theological ferment of the mid–sixteenth century and a reflection of the spiritual fervor of the time, a time when the scriptures in the vernacular were providing ordinary people with an exhilarating insight into their faith. It is significant, therefore, that these homilies are at pains to identify the relationship between a faith received as a gift, assuring the believer of forgiveness and reconciliation with God through the mediating work of Christ and the indwelling work of the Spirit, and what this meant for daily Christian living in the world. On the one hand they affirmed a radical doctrine of justification, which declared God's grace to be all things and human effort nothing; on the other hand they propounded a sense of the created order of the world from which God had by no means completely withdrawn, and in which the efficacy of Christ's atonement did not diminish the need to practice ordinary good works in the rough and tumble of daily living.

Salvation, Faith, and Good Works

In the homilies on salvation, faith, and good works, the outcome is a carefully crafted dialectic between grace and obligation.

First, the doctrine of grace:

> Because all men are sinners against God, and breakers of his law, therefore can no man by his works be justified, and made righteous before God. But every man is constrained to seek for another righteousness or justification, to be received at God's own hands. And this . . . which we receive of God's mercy, and Christ's merits embraced by faith, is taken, accepted and allowed of God, for our perfect and full justification. . . . And because this is wrought through the only merits of Christ, and not through our merits, or through the merit of any virtue we have within us, or of any work that cometh from us: Therefore in that respect, we renounce as it were, again, faith, works and all other virtues. For our corruption through original sin is so great, that all our faith, charity, words and works cannot merit or deserve any part of our justification for us. And therefore we thus speak, humbling ourselves to God, and giving to our Saviour Christ all the glory of our justification.[9]

But then comes the law, in equal measure:

> It is diligently to be noted, that faith is taken in Scripture two ways: There is one faith, which the Scripture calleth a dead faith; and this, by St. James is compared to the faith of devils, who believe and tremble, and yet do nothing well: and such a faith as this have wicked Christians, who profess they know God, but in works deny him. . . . Another faith there is in Scripture, which is not idle or unfruitful, but (as St. Paul declares) working by love. [This faith] is not in the mouth, and outward profession only, but it liveth and stirreth inwardly in the heart: and this faith is not without hope and trust in God, nor without the love of God, and of our neighbour, nor without the fear of God, nor without the desire to hear God's Word, and to follow the same, in avoiding evil, and gladly doing all good works.[10]

And finally, a statement of God's universal grace, as the necessary context for faith, works, and justification alike:

> Wherefore, as ye have any regard for everlasting life, apply yourselves above all things to read and hear God's word, mark diligently what his commandments are, and with all your endeavour follow the same. First, you must have an assured faith in God, and give yourselves wholly unto him; love him in prosperity and adversity, and dread to offend him evermore. Then for his sake, love all men, friends and foes, because they are his creatures and image, and redeemed by Christ as ye are.[11]

The dialectic is poignant, because Thomas Cranmer, Archbishop of Canterbury and architect of these *Homilies,* was one of the sixteenth-century martyrs who did not debate such things lightly. The statements make clear that, from the beginning of English Protestant thought, there was a recognition that God's grace was not limited to a justifying faith. In the following century, in large measure in response to the strictures of a hardened TULIP formula emanating from the Synod of Dort,[12] this was articulated more specifically in the doctrine of prevenient grace. As one Anglican scholar put it, "You are mistaken when you think the Doctrine of Universall Redemption Arminianisme. It was the doctrine of the Church of England before Arminius was born. We learned it out of the old Church Catechisme."[13]

The Doctrine of Prevenient Grace

The theologian who did most to tradition this doctrine is better known as an evangelist and founder of Methodism, the Anglican cleric

John Wesley. Yet his theology, honed in the exigencies of preaching
the gospel to ordinary people the length and breadth of the land, is
perhaps on this very count the most reliable of any key Protestant
leader. As Wesley traditioned prevenient grace, it was not a denial of
human depravity after the fall, but rather that the *present* state of
human nature is not one of total depravity. God has subsequently
bequeathed to every human being a measure of responsibility, so that
the "natural" human condition is also one of grace. A natural conscience
has been restored to humanity, "more properly termed 'preventing
grace.'" And of this, "no [one] living is entirely destitute."[14]

The implications are profound. By prevenient grace, indwelling and
universal, we are drawn to saving grace. By the same prevenient grace,
indwelling and universal, we are given the freedom to resist saving
grace. And thus is resolved the "disjunction between nature and grace
. . . that philosophical and theological ineptitude of the Reformation."[15]

A Christ-Centered Discipleship

What can we infer from this for our Christian discipleship? First, that
our identity as Christians gives us the privilege of a particular grace,
but that this must not place us in a Christian penthouse, nor yet in a
Christian ghetto. God's grace is at work in the whole of humankind, as
is God's justice, and both will have an eschatological fulfillment in
which the sole advantage of the Christian will be that of advanced
knowledge and foretaste. Indeed, having been given the particular
privilege of the firstfruits of the reign of God, Christians will be the
more particularly accountable for how they have used the talents
thereby entrusted to them.

Just as important is the inference that our Christian discipleship
must draw, not on a gospel that is faith-centered, but on one that is
Christ-centered. If Cushman's diagnosis makes one thing clear, it is
that the Reformation engendered a hermeneutic which did quite the
opposite, and thereby rendered our discipleship a matter of personal
preoccupation. And so perforce it will be, as long as faith in Christ
rather than Christ is the center of our spiritual understanding—the
anthropocentric aberration which ironically denies the incarnational
presence of God in humanity as a whole.

Once this aberration is clear, the scriptural referents spring from the
page. Take, for example, the contrast between the spontaneity and

informality of Jesus' meeting with the children of Salem, or the woman at the well, or even the rich young ruler, and then the forced intentionality which so often emanates from a concern to get our, and everyone else's, faith right. While we busy ourselves trying to get people to respond to the gospel the way we want them to (i.e., the way they *ought* to), it is little wonder that the immediate needs of those who suffer in the world are frequently relegated to the category of theological enquiry. While the goats of Matthew 25 debate whether or how to help Christ's little ones as an appropriate act of discipleship, so often it is those claiming to have no discipleship, but with much prevenient grace, who get on with the job.

All of which brings us back to the question of Christian identity. For if God's grace is universally prevenient, then what demands can the gospel legitimately make of anyone? Why be a Christian, giving our time and energy to congregations which so often prove to be chronically self-centered, and for a gospel which so often seems impotent in the face of human suffering? Does Christian faith have any advantage at all over the best of human wisdom, if human wisdom is no less graciously God-given?

Nor are these questions merely academic. They are asked week after week by countless dedicated disciples, striving to find integrity in their commitment to Christ through what seem to be countless detours. The answer lies in the word *obedience*. Given the universality of grace, the only authentic Christian calling is that which comes directly from Christ, the risen Christ, and which commissions us as channels of God's saving-righteousness to help with the leavening of the world.

Ours is not to save the world, but to impart to the world our knowledge of the coming reign of God, and to help prepare for its fullness. Ours it is to be available to serve, at particular times and places, the One who has called us to be disciplined helpers, as God's Spirit continues to bring planet Earth back to its rightful place in the Cosmos. The fullness of that salvation is yet to be revealed; but Christians have a most particular part to play in the final preparations. To play that part requires, not the largess of ultimate knowledge, nor the zeal of professional life-saving, nor yet the pomposity of an enlightened life-style. All of these betoken little more than the soteriological bad manners we have already censured. Rather it requires of us the childlike trust which impels us to take to the world an outrageously hopeful message: that God was in Christ, reconciling the world, and inaugurating a new age which will come to fulfillment through the power of the Holy Spirit, in whose work we are privileged to share.

The Blockage Identified

Having discerned that the source of our ecclesial blockage is an anthropocentric inversion of the gospel, we can now proceed to identify the blockage itself: Salvation and discipleship are not the same thing, and our confusion of the two is the cause of our enervating centripetal inertia. Salvation is what Christ has done for us, unilaterally and unequivocally. All that is required of us is to accept it as a given, a gracious gift. And though we still must decide to accept it, this is not a proactive choice, but one that is submissive. We do not choose to accept the saving work of Christ: We finally make the decision not to reject it. It is the "zero-point" of our will,[16] the critical moment of surrender when we decide not to say no to grace:

> His love is mighty to compel;
> His conqu'ring love consent to feel,
> Yield to his love's resistless power,
> And fight against your God no more.[17]

The scriptural witness further testifies that God will pursue us with this grace into all eternity. We refuse it at our peril, for God's judgment is also eternal. But likewise there will always be grace, to bring Christ's long, slow victory to fulfillment. Placing limitations or restrictions on this is not only a misunderstanding of the scriptural concepts of time. It is also to usurp the divine prerogative, and to presume to foreclose on the divine search being conducted in the wilderness for lost sheep, as well as the business being transacted with unworthy servants in the divine woodshed, through the keyhole of which no one will ever be allowed to peep. Eternal reckoning there will be; there must be. But in keeping with the divine nature, such reckoning is bound to be remedial.

Personal Salvation

Our salvation, therefore, is not in our own hands. It is a divine fiat. And while it carries an invitation, it is an invitation to accept something which cannot be changed. It is the divine *krisis*, an ultimatum with an awful inevitability. For this is a salvation that is going to prevail, all worldly resistance and procrastination notwithstanding.

We do not, therefore, invite people to be saved. That is a travesty of grace, which turns the cross into little more than the opportunity to negotiate an advantageous arrangement. Rather, we inform them of their salvation, and suggest that, since the new age of Jesus Christ is already here and imminently to be fulfilled, this is a reality they would be well advised to accept—right now. For in this new age of God's *basileia*, the retention of sinful bad habits will cause a marked degree of discomfort.

Systemic Salvation

Our announcement of the *basileia* as God's *fait accompli* carries a further implication: A new order is coming to planet Earth, God's *oikonomia*.[18] It calls us to accept the efficacy of God's grace, not only in persons, but also in societies. It calls us not only to denounce injustice and oppression, but also to pronounce God's salvation for the systems of the world. It means that we regard worldly power not only in terms of its abuse, but also in terms of its redemption by God for the new age. And more, it means being ready to accept the firstfruits of this redemption when we see them.[19]

In other words, the *evangel* must have as full a message of God's salvation for systems as for individuals. Communities, cities, nations, conglomerates, must not only be denounced as sinful, but must also be pronounced saved, and called to repentance and conversion no less than persons. Moreover, they can be expected to repent (Jon. 3:5ff.; Matt. 11:20-24, 12:41-42). For their salvation, along with that of individuals, will be nurtured and brought to fulfillment by the love and the grace of God.

A Truncated Gospel

Our confusion of salvation with discipleship has tended to truncate this vital dimension of the gospel, and thereby restrict our evangelism to an overpersonalized message. Furthermore, instead of impelling Christians into the world with a universal love for their planet, it has fostered a subtle alienation. For if the gospel, which challenges the systems in which people live and work, is seen to lack the redemptive grace with which they are personally called to repentance and conversion, then people will continue to view their own salvation separately from that of the world. Whereas if their salvation extends beyond themselves to their social and global setting, and if God's grace can be seen at work in every dimension of human existence, then the gospel can be understood as a truly universal message of hope—which, of course, is precisely what we find in the sayings and promises of Jesus.

All of this we can announce with confidence, because of the Jew, Jesus of Nazareth. He is God's gift to humanity, and he has accomplished our salvation, a salvation we need only accept. It is free. It is done. And how do we know this? God raised him from the dead on the third day.

The Invitation to Discipleship

Discipleship, on the other hand, is very much a proactive choice, and the invitation will always be extended with conditions. The great spiritual writer Oswald Chambers puts it this way:

> There is nothing easier than getting saved because it is God's sovereign work—Come unto Me and I will save you. Our Lord never lays down the conditions of discipleship as the conditions of salvation. We are condemned to salvation through the Cross of Jesus Christ. Discipleship has an option with it—"IF any one . . ."[20]

It is this "if" which distinguishes between salvation and discipleship: the one a free gift for all, the other a costly commitment. And once we have made this distinction, we see why we have such a blockage of God's grace in our contemporary congregational life. By attaching the conditions of discipleship to salvation, we overload the doctrine of justification, and weight its efficacy on our faith response to Christ rather than on what Christ has done for us.

Soteriological Impediments

In effect, we make it very difficult to be saved, because we insist on a particular faith experience in order to receive salvation.[21] For those who are able to enter into such an experience, and especially when it is focused on a critical conversion, there is the deep inward assurance traditionally known as "being saved." But by the same token, the doubts and uncertainties which inevitably occur in the Christian life can be correspondingly unnerving for such persons, and can even lead to religious neuroses as they wonder whether their lack of assurance means that they are now "unsaved."

The number of North American Christians with this confused understanding of salvation and discipleship is considerable, and the fact that it remains an unexamined assumption in large parts of the church inhibits many sensitive persons from claiming the gift of their salvation at all, on the grounds of inadequate spiritual experience. In effect, faith is made into a work, something the Anglican *Homilies* clearly refuted, and which is by no means the doctrinal substance of God's forgiveness and reconciliation. The reality of our salvation is that Christ has accomplished it for us, whenever we happen to accept it, and whether or not we happen to feel it or believe it at any given moment.

Passive Discipleship

There is another unfortunate effect of confusing salvation with discipleship. In order to have these two concepts conflate, we find ourselves presenting discipleship in a predominantly passive mode— the "mind-set" response we critiqued at the outset of our study.[22] Of course, we encourage a life-style appropriate for Christian persons. But once we have identified discipleship with salvation, it is very difficult to press the claims of a Christian life-style. Inevitably, discipleship becomes mere belief in Jesus Christ and acceptance of his atoning work, with Christlike living a series of options. And though it is hoped that these options will be exercised as far as possible, they are by no means viewed as necessities.[23]

This has the effect of rendering cheap the invitation to discipleship which Jesus made clear was very costly indeed. For the last thing we can ask of people who are at the point of repentance and forgiveness is that they do something to earn their reconciliation with God. That would be to place a price tag on Christ's atoning passion and God's grace, both of which are free. Yet if we have identified becoming a disciple with this critical surrender to grace, on what grounds can we then talk about the "cost of discipleship" (Luke 14:25ff.)? It might be argued that this is a matter of subsequent obligation, were it not for Jesus' insistence that disciples consider the cost *before* making their commitment, clearly indicating that discipleship is by direct invitation, not enticement. Future obligations there will be; but the call is to be answered with a readiness to serve, not a weighing of the benefits.

The only way we can retain the integrity of free salvation and costly discipleship, therefore, is to keep them very distinct. They are inextricably linked; but they are by no means the same.

Diffident Discipleship

Yet another unfortunate effect of confusing these two dimensions of the Christian life is that persons in our congregations who are ready to pay the price of discipleship will hold back from such a commitment for no other reason than the unreadiness of their neighborly Christians to do likewise. Their reluctance is quite understandable. If discipleship and salvation are synonymous, even incipiently so, then to advance in discipleship is to imply a greater degree of salvation. And since this for obvious reasons is distasteful (a point to be kept very much in mind when considering who is "saved" as opposed to "unsaved"), potentially dedicated disciples are hesitant about getting ahead of their Christian friends and neighbors.

As we have noted, this is usually rationalized by presenting discipleship as a wide range of personal options, the very thing that makes it so vulnerable to late-twentieth-century Western enculturation. For in this diffusion of Christian commitment, the small deed is extolled just as much as the large. The person who makes a sacrificial commitment of time, skills, and resources is regarded as exercising a choice of life-style, neither more nor less Christlike than the person who engages in peripheral churchly activities. In terms of their salvation, of course, there is no distinction at all between these persons. But in terms of their discipleship, to deny the difference between their commitments is not only to fly in the face of reality. It is also to play havoc with our accountability as servants of Jesus Christ. Even allowing for the legitimate vicissitudes of stewardship, and likewise taking care not to slip into judgments over motes and beams, such an equalizing of Christian discipleship in the lavishly endowed culture of contemporary North America is patently perverse. It penalizes congregational life with diffidence and disdain.

A False Dichotomy

Theologically, what all of this means is that we have changed the doctrine of justification by grace through faith into justification by faith. As Christian disciples commissioned to evangelize the world, that leaves us with a false dichotomy in our perceptions of humanity: those who have faith in Christ, and those who do not. Salvation becomes so predominantly a question of faith—and to be candid, the sort of faith we as Christians determine to be appropriate—that we project a version of the gospel which is contingent on these false options.

People are "saved" or "not saved." They are home and dry, or they are beyond the pale. At least, this is how it often comes across. And since this goes against the better instincts of most of our church members, evangelism becomes an embarrassing part of our congregational life and work, avoided by many, and undertaken with all the greater zeal by those who feel the urgency of "making disciples," which is to say, "saving souls." The result is that evangelism is typed as an activity for some, but not for others. It is perceived as a ministry requiring a special kind of religious experience, and has thus become a divisive issue in many parts of the North American church.

Degrees of Faith

We have already referred to John Wesley as a trustworthy theologian on account of his lifetime's work among ordinary folk, and it is helpful at this point to return to his writings for further illumination. As we follow his *Journal* for the years 1738 to 1740, we find that he wrestled at great length with the doctrine of justification at the outset of his evangelistic ministry.[24] We also find that his enquiries led him to a confrontation with his spiritual mentors, the Moravians, over this very issue of salvation and discipleship.

It took place at the Fetter Lane Society in London, which he had helped to found. On his return to the society following a visit to Bristol in the June of 1740, he was horrified to find what he described as a "leaving off [of] good works in order to an increase of faith."[25] The issue was that of "quietism" over against what Wesley understood to be "degrees of faith." Under Moravian influence, and especially that of Philip Molther, society members were waiting for the full assurance of faith, and regarding "weak faith" as no faith at all. Moreover, since this "full faith" could only be received as a gracious gift from God, any kind of works—good works for Christ among the poor, and even the ordinances of the church—were to be laid aside pending the divine initiative in their lives.[26]

As Wesley pointed out, however, there are different ways of waiting. To wait quietly and inactively, believing that only with a particular fullness of faith could one's life be pleasing to God, was a false alternative of the most pernicious kind. Good works, works meet for repentance, the means of grace (prayer, Bible reading, worship, the ministries of word and sacrament), all of these could help a person to serve Jesus Christ while waiting for the full assurance of faith. Indeed, was this not what Christ told us to do? That *by* feeding the hungry, visiting the prisons, and using the means of grace, faith could not only be strengthened, but received (Matt. 21:28-32, 25:44-46)?[27]

Wesley's contact with ordinary people had tuned his instincts well. There was no one more convinced than he of the efficacy and significance of religious experience. He was, after all, the one whose heart had been "strangely warmed" at Aldersgate Street only two years earlier.[28] But he also saw the grace of God at work in people's lives with infinite variety. He saw faith being conceived, birthed, and nurtured in ways no theological or spiritual principles could in any way delineate. A Christ-centered gospel would always allow people to respond in their own way and in their own time with whatever measure of grace the Holy Spirit would extend. A faith-centered gospel, on the other hand, would impose a false dichotomy on these responses, and judge them acceptable or not.[29]

Degrees of Response

If we agree with Wesley that there are "degrees of faith," then we must also accept that a person's response to the gospel cannot be the measure of that person's salvation. To suggest that Jesus was "more or less crucified" is clearly an offensive proposition. Yet just as clearly, people respond to the critical challenge of the cross in different ways and at different times.

Accordingly, the nature of their response cannot be the ultimate evangelistic concern of the church. It is our business to cultivate such response; to seek it, encourage it, and above all to nurture it into full acceptance of the grace of God. But it is not our business to evaluate it. If we try to do so, we will almost certainly get it wrong. By the same token, we can never deny a relationship with God to those who may not be Christians, but who, with sensitive perception and with much prevenient grace, are seeing what the Holy Spirit is doing in the world, and responding accordingly.

If God's salvation is being worked out through the risen Christ, who is universally present in and through the power of the Holy Spirit, then the purpose of our evangelism is to declare the Good News of that salvation to the world. We inform people about their salvation. We anticipate their response with whatever degree of grace and faith God gives them, and as the church, we gather and build them up in the faith. Then, as we sense the call in ourselves and others, we further invite those who are ready to make the more costly commitment to help the risen Christ prepare for the fullness of God's salvation, on earth as in heaven. And these we call Christian disciples.

A Christ-Centered Evangelism

All of which perforce requires us to evangelize with a Christ-centeredness, not a faith-centeredness. This is not to deny the significance of studies in faith development. The work of Kohlberg, Fowler, and others has been an important breakthrough in our pastoral ministry.[30] But while faith understandings can *inform* our evangelism, they cannot substitute for the *evangel*, any more than the theological reflection which hones the gospel can govern its content. The whole point of the gospel is that it must be proclaimed to all persons without bias. For no scripture, no teaching, no church, no council, no congregation, no preacher, no priest, no human pronouncement whatsoever can make *any* determination about how God will judge another human being.

The gospel makes it clear that God so loved the world that Jesus died for everyone's salvation. The only appropriate attitude for our evangelism, therefore, is one of universal hope. Christ died for us while we were still sinners. There is no way out. We *must* sit at the table. We must mend our manners, and sit next to whomever God assigns us. As the seventeenth-century covenant prayer eloquently expresses it, "Put me to what thou wilt; rank me with whom thou wilt."[31] This is the real offense of the gospel, because the truth of the human condition is that we *don't* want to be saved. We prefer the self-justification and irresponsibility of our sin to God's justification and the accountability of our salvation. Which is why any evangelism implying that salvation is a way of avoiding accountability is a serious mistake.

Does this mean, then, that there is no invitation to be made as we share the gospel; that we merely inform people of what Christ has done? Not at all. But the invitation to accept the saving-righteousness of God and the invitation to become a disciple of Jesus Christ are very different indeed, in emphasis and in presentation. The first is not so much an invitation to make a decision or take an initiative, as it is the declaration of a reality that needs to be unconcealed in people's lives and the world in which they live.[32] We inform people of their salvation, accomplished for them already by Jesus Christ, in such a way that the invitation to repent and come home to God, to accept their status as children of God, is a recommendation to exercise minimal common sense. We *are* the children of God, so we all need to accept the code of manners befitting the coming reign of God.

The invitation we extend to Christian discipleship, on the other hand, is at once more intentional and demanding. The cost is made clear, and the conditions presented up front. To accept it will mean a radical change in our priorities, and a commitment to following Jesus Christ every step of the way—if need be, to the cross itself.

When this distinction is clear, our message of Good News is authentic, and God's universal grace can flow to all the world. As we have maintained throughout, the channels of the North American church have considerable capacity for precisely such a flow. It remains now to examine the implications of having them cleared: first, what it means for the role of the church in the world; and then, what it means for the life and work of the local congregation.

CONGREGATIONS AND DISCIPLES: QUESTIONS OF IDENTITY

Congregational Implications

Having drawn a distinction between salvation and discipleship as a means of clearing our present blockage of grace in the North American church, we must now ask what it will mean to have the blockage cleared. What will be the effect in congregations when the gospel flows freely through these communities of faith to do its work in the world? Even more pertinent to our enquiry, what place in congregations is there for committed disciples, the kind of Christians who composed the house *ekklēsia* of the primitive church?

Ecclesial Identity

All of these questions require us to look again at the issue of Christian identity we examined in the last chapter, but this time against the backdrop of the church. For if we accept that there are degrees of faith and varying levels of commitment among those who believe in the saving work of Jesus Christ, then not only must we consider the place of disciplined disciples in the spectrum of the Christian community. We must likewise be clear about the role of the church in the spectrum of humanity—God's global community.

We have already determined that becoming a Christian and joining the church is not the only response to grace; that there are other ways of working for the coming reign of Jesus Christ which, in the larger plan of God's salvation, are not only appropriate, but are also as much

115

a work of grace as Christian discipleship. This is in no way to deny the uniqueness of Jesus Christ as Savior of the world. On the contrary, it is to make his work truly universal. For when the church proclaims that Jesus Christ is Savior of the world, it will perforce be pointing to a *basileia* infinitely more righteous and a *shalom* infinitely more pervasive than its own embodiment of the gospel, important though this might be as a foretaste of that which is to come.

The problem is that the church regularly and mistakenly identifies itself with this *basileia*, albeit with temporal limitations, and thereby projects the ambition of ultimately becoming a salvific community of all peoples. This engenders an ecclesiocentric evangelism, which is designed primarily to gather everyone into Christian "safe-houses," and which therefore tends to avoid those dimensions of the gospel that might seem to deter or impede such a process. In order to maximize a particular response (i.e., the churchly response), the gospel is adapted to the cultural norms of the society in which the church happens to find itself. As the Uruguayan theologian Juan Luis Segundo has observed:

> If the community called Church wanted to be the community of all mankind, or at least of the majority of mankind, it would have to take the line of least resistance and make it as easy as possible for people.[1]

And this, we have suggested, is precisely what we find today in so much of the North American church.

A Particular Sign Community

In his highly significant 5-volume study of the Christian life, *Artisans of a New Humanity*, Segundo argues that the church, far from being a universal community, is very particular indeed. Its identity is based on the life, death, and resurrection of the Christ, who is also Jesus of Nazareth. Just as the particularity of this event prevents the human race from projecting its own limitations onto God, so it prevents the church from projecting its limitations onto God's saving-righteousness. The fact of the matter is that the incarnation of God in Jesus of Nazareth established once and for all that the whole of humanity is on a common journey toward God's salvation. It must therefore be concluded that "at least in some cases the Church (i.e., visible membership in the Christian community) is not always and everywhere the ideal situation with respect to salvation for all."[2]

The question thus becomes, What is distinctively Christian in this human journey? What is the identity of this particular community of faith? The answer is that a number of people on this common road know, through revelation, something that relates to all. They know the mystery of the journey. And what they know, they know in order to make a contribution to the common quest. The church is the community of those who, within the divine plan that is common to all humanity, are entrusted through the revelation of the Christ event with an understanding of what is really happening in and to the world—a "sign community" among the pluralism of God's saving activities in the world.

This identity is at once salutary and liberating for the church. It is salutary in its implication that the church cannot regard itself as the community of the saved—the desire to be the *locus* of the coming reign of God rather than its herald.[3] It is highly instructive for the Christian to look into the world for the hope of God's salvation, and to accept the relevance and necessity of such discoveries for the nature and content of the *evangel*. Likewise it is liberating to find God's salvation operative beyond the Christian community; liberating in that it frees the Christian for the fuller vision of the elective commission of God, which lies beyond the parochialisms of privatized salvation; liberating also in that it absolves the Christian from the two-kingdoms riddle of being in, yet not of the world. There is fostered instead the reality of being wholly in *and* of the world, yet knowing that a new age is already present and imminently to be fulfilled.[4]

Evangelistic Inversions

This requires what in many instances must be an inversion of prevailing evangelistic concepts. It means that the church must acknowledge the universality of God's grace already at work in the world, and accept that this work is not merely a "warming-up of the audience" for the evangelist. It is rather a co-equal force in the work of God's salvation. When we evangelize, we do not offer people Christ: We inform them that Christ has died for them; and more, is already present in their lives through the prevenient, universal grace of the Holy Spirit. Our doctrine of the Trinity declares this to be so, and we must evangelize with nothing less.

Such a reversal of evangelistic concepts will require a similarly drastic revision in most of our contemporary evangelistic practice. Although the theological groundwork for this has been laid in the past two decades by a number of writers,[5] and though we have at least one set of denominational resources which comes to grips with these issues,[6] much remains to be done in the development of strategies congregations can use in making the necessary changes in their evangelistic ministry. Mere expression of concern for the social and universal dimensions of the gospel will not suffice so long as the models in use remain personalized and aimed primarily at membership recruitment for the church. There must be a fundamental shift, both in emphasis and in direction.

Evangelization by the World

The identity of the church as sign community further means acknowledging that this same universal grace, present among all peoples, all cultures, and to a quite remarkable degree among all religions, can be a means of evangelizing the church no less than the gospel is a means of evangelizing the world.[7] Once again, this is not to deny the uniqueness of Christ as the Savior of the world, but merely to give due emphasis to the whole of his salvific title. Yes, Christ is Savior; but Savior of the *world*, not just Christians. God's salvation in Christ is not limited to the church, any more than it is limited to Israel.[8] To invert a well-known saying of John Wesley, the world is not our parish—our parish is the world.[9]

Accordingly, there will be times when the church needs to listen to what the world has to say about the coming riegn of God. This may happen individually, as Christians are informed and illumined by insights of people whose knowledge of the gospel, or even of things religious, is quite minimal, but whose integrity and honor and love are self-evident works of grace. It may also happen institutionally, where basic good manners and a vital concern for justice, especially where it concerns the poor and the victimized, are quite often evinced more readily by public officials and politicians than by church leaders.

This is not to suggest that the church does not have a mission and ministry to the world. But it is to say that the church receives a great deal from the world in addition to what it gives. For much of the progress toward the reign of God in human society emanates directly from the universal grace of God, and only indirectly from the work of the church. Even when the catalyst for such change is the church, it tends to be through Christian influences rather than Christian actions. The Holy Spirit makes this a regular practice, lest the servants of God presume to take undue credit.

In the field of interfaith dialogue, this two-way work of grace is known as "mutual evangelization"—an openness to the Holy Spirit at work in other persons and other religions.[10] The Christian evangelist must be ready to learn something new about God (and therefore about Christ) through the faith of others, whatever that faith might be. And since the gospel proclaims Christ to be God incarnate, the only risk in such a process is that of possible correction and illumination for the Christian. The veracity of the gospel is not at risk at all, since that would be a contradiction in terms.[11]

Such evangelistic risk is no less valid and applicable in the area of congregational life and work. Indeed, for church folk to be as open to seeing God's grace at work in their neighborly pagan as they are to seeking it in their Christian community would be a refreshing affirmation of the gospel. And just as important, it would be very effective evangelism.

Elected for Christ

Accordingly, the identity of the church is very particular indeed. The church is to be a catalytic agent of the Holy Spirit in a plan of salvation having many dimensions. Its task is to serve Jesus Christ faithfully; to wait expectantly; and to declare as often as possible, to as many as possible, in as many ways as possible, the reality of realities—that Jesus Christ will return to fulfill God's redemption of the world in a final triumph over sin, evil, and death. As it does so, it will inexorably perceive and affirm the infinite variety of God's grace in the world.

It follows that membership in such a church can only be elective; an election, as we have already noted, into covenant with God.[12] This covenant, the bedrock of Israel, was renewed and definitively established in Jesus of Nazareth, crucified, dead, and raised from the dead. It is therefore Jesus who must be extolled at the center of all things properly Christian—the "flaming center."[13] Only when Christ pervades its life, its work, and above all its message, will the church function as the church.

Discipleship and the Church

Yet once this is stated, our question becomes even more pressing: How do we ensure that the church is Christ-centered? And more, What do we do with a church that is enculturated to the point where it is a very mixed community indeed, and where costly discipleship seems to be all too rare? Must we declare such a church to be apostate, and focus our pastoral energies on the few who are ready to count the cost and pay the price of a disciplined discipleship? Or is it possible to have a more positive view of the larger ecclesial community, cultural proclivities and assimilations notwithstanding?

It is something of a relief to find that this question is by no means new. Indeed, it appears to have been the predicament of faithful Christian disciples and churchly institutions alike in every generation. That the church is always in need of reform *(ecclesia semper reformanda est)* is no mere sophism. It is a Christic *cri de coeur*. For when so much remains to be done to prepare for the coming reign of God Jesus promised, it is a mystery that the church should be so caught up with its own welfare. It is an enigma of the first order that the community Jesus called to be his particular continuing embodiment in the world, to be a sign of God's coming *shalom*, should so often align itself with the way things are rather than the way Christ promised they would be.

A Recurring Tension

Even a cursory glance at the history of Christianity reveals this recurring tension between the spirit of dynamic discipleship and the structured order and doctrine of the church. Much of the time the tension has been healthy, and not infrequently it has been through the very affirmation of the doctrines and ordinances of the church that costly discipleship has been exercised.[14] More often, however, we find that the Holy Spirit has worked through faithful disciples, as individuals, groups, or movements, to reform and renew the institutional church.

This is not to suggest that ecclesial institutions are inherently bereft of grace. Indeed, our argument thus far requires us to state the contrary: that God is at work in churchly structures no less than in dynamic spiritual movements, just as God's grace is to be found throughout the world as well as in the church. But it is to observe that those who devote their lives to a disciplined discipleship, in a direct relationship of obedience to Jesus Christ, time and again find that their role is to have a reforming influence on the church—no less than the impact they might have on the world, and sometimes much more.

Agents of Churchly Reform

The pattern of this reform seems to have two basic characteristics. On the one hand, those who are called to such a task make it a priority to have a spiritually disciplined walk with Christ. This being so, they seek to know God for God's own sake. They delight in those spiritual practices which take them into the presence of God. They know the power of prayer. They drink from the wellspring of the scriptures. They feed on the liturgies and sacraments of the church. They build one another up through Christian conference, intentionally questing for the will of God in the company of like-minded Christian colleagues. And most important of all, they take the time to contemplate and meditate on God's truth. As Robin Maas has put it, they keep their appointments with God, and thus learn more of the mind of God.[15]

By the same token, their discipleship takes on the shape and form of the ministry of Jesus of Nazareth. Being spiritual, they are also incarnational. They live out the teachings of Jesus in a very practical way, which means that they find themselves drawn into the same circles in which Jesus moved. As they do so, they are moved by compassion to feed the hungry, clothe the naked, visit the imprisoned, and minister to the oppressed and the marginalized of human society. This in turn opens their eyes to the injustices of the world, and impels them into solidarity with the poor and the helpless. They find growing in themselves the same divine bias with which the Old Testament prophets declared God's outrage at the suffering of the world's little ones. They become angry, and vociferous, and not always good company in ecclesial safe-houses.

The second dimension of their reforming influence is that these disciplined disciples ultimately drive the church back into the world. This might seem to be a contradiction, in that cultural conformity engendered by worldly involvement is so often what occasions the need for ecclesial reform. But there is a difference. The impulse of a church empowered by the Holy Spirit is to announce, prepare for, and exemplify the coming reign of God. It is to be a subversive agent of Jesus Christ, and a transforming agent of the Holy Spirit.[16]

Authentic discipleship never invites the church to an other-worldly plane of existence, therefore, but rather reinforces its worldly presence as God's clear sign of that which is to come—a new age of love and justice and peace for a redeemed people on a redeemed planet.

Influences and Rejections

When the church has been receptive to such influences, these disciples have not only been given a hearing: They have been recognized as mentors and guides, as teachers and role models. At such times, the church has become increasingly Christ-centered, for the simple reason that its leadership has been Christ-centered—all other members, whatever their stage of faith or depth of commitment, taking their cue from the life-style these leaders have evinced. As a Christ-centered institution *in* the world, the church has thus been a rich and powerful means of grace *for* the world. It has fulfilled the mandate of Christ to be light, and salt, and leaven, and seed (Matt. 5:13-16, 13:31-33). Being centered on Christ, it has been unavoidably committed to the coming reign of God.

There are many times, however, when the church has refused to acknowledge such disciples as its leaders. Not only have they then been ignored, but also their leadership has passed to ecclesial and even political hierarchies, the results of which have all too often been an evangelistic stagnation and a religious and cultural blockage of grace. To the extent that these disciples have challenged the ecclesial hierarchy of the day, either through their deep spiritual devotion to God (something which always cuts to the quick when it confronts those who claim to represent God, but rarely spend time in God's presence), or through their deep solidarity with the poor and the outcasts (something which not only draws attention to God's justice in society at large, but discomforts those with ecclesial power who have made a premature peace with the world), they have found themselves reviled, persecuted, and even put to death (Matt. 5:10-12, 10:16ff.; Luke 21:16). It is a tragedy of the church that the persecution of disciplined disciples has so often been aided, abetted, and even perpetrated by the ecclesial powers of the day. Thus it was with Jesus himself; and thus it has been time and again throughout the centuries of Christian history.

Institutional Renewal

It is tempting to infer from these persecutions that reform and renewal in the Christian community will inevitably place churchly institutions and faithful disciples at loggerheads. From such a standpoint, ecclesial hierarchies are seen as socioreligious power structures against which the claims of God's justice must be pronounced by authentic disciples, whose task is to be the true *ekklēsia* of Jesus Christ in the midst of unjust societies and compromised churches. From the same standpoint, congregations of the church are viewed as socioreligious communities who must be shown the true meaning of spiritual communion with God by genuine disciples, whose privilege it is to be the true *agapē-koinonia* of the Holy Spirit in the midst of pagan societies and nominal Christians.

When we examine times of renewal throughout the history of the church, however, this mutual antipathy is by no means consistent.[17] In fact, there is only one constant in the dynamic of churchly reform: its unpredictability. Times of ecclesial vitality and vigorous propagation of the gospel cannot be forecast, any more than the persecutions of faithful disciples can be rationalized. Beelzebul will attack on whichever front there seems to be a weakness in the ranks of the servants of God, and any attempt to analyze these skirmishes is fraught with historiographical pitfalls.[18] More important, such analyses, albeit enhanced today by the disciplines of social anthropology and psychology, tend to underestimate the seductive skill of the powers and principalities of this world in diverting faithful Christian disciples from the task in hand.

These diversions emerged quite clearly when we considered the dilemma of our discipleship today.[19] Concern for the renewal of the church, we found, can easily become an end in itself, and lead to the use of spiritual amphetamines. Concern for social justice can likewise veer toward a utopianism that neglects to focus on the one true source of the coming reign of God. In each case, the church is diverted to an egotistical course, in which the questions being asked are predominantly anthropocentric: How do we foster a congregational setting in which the inward spiritual needs of the believer are more effectively nurtured? And how do we focus our congregational life on ministries of justice and love that will initiate social change?

Christ-Centered Questions

With our ecclesial blockage cleared, however, and a truly universal grace flowing through our kerygmatic arteries, we can ask these same questions differently. How do we focus the spiritual life of our congregations on the person and ministry of Jesus Christ? And how do we pattern our congregational outreach on the coming reign of Jesus Christ? Once we pose the questions in this way, the history of ecclesial reform is rich with answers, and the tension between costly discipleship and the institutional church becomes an invigorating interplay. We find the issues to be precisely those which have been asked by faithful disciples in every generation, as they have yearned for the coming reign of God on earth as in heaven. Through their radical devotion, they have witnessed to God's righteousness in the world; and through their radical stand for God's justice in the world, they have witnessed to the depth of their spiritual communion with God. When the church has heard them and followed them—which not infrequently it has—then it has served the risen Christ more faithfully and effectively. And even when it has rejected and persecuted them, their witness and their sacrifice have never been in vain.

This is not the place for a detailed historical analysis. But in order not to leave these observations merely abstract, we can cite a few nuggets which glisten in the annals of Protestantism; and for a modern case study, we can draw from the Roman Catholic tradition.

Reforming Agents: (1) Early Reformation

Our first example is a representative expression of the tremendous surge of freedom which came with the early Protestant Reformation. In large measure, this was due to the radical formulation of the doctrine of justification; and though it was necessary in an earlier chapter to provide a course correction for some of the doctrine's theological implications,[20] we must not allow this to detract from the critical and at times euphoric affirmation of those decades—that every sinner is made righteous by the grace of Jesus Christ, and stands justified before God, *coram Deo*, through the grace of Jesus Christ, through no personal merit at all. However misguided the church subsequently may have been in working out this doctrine of salvation, it has freed us once and for all from ecclesial oppression.

Yet another freedom won for us in those years was that of access to the scriptures. Once again, it is a freedom that has not always been exercised responsibly, but that does not diminish the significance of having the authoritative witness of the church in our own hands and our own language.

All of which makes the following testimony ring powerfully down the ages:

> But at last I heard speak of Jesus, even then when the New Testament was first set forth by Erasmus; which when I understood to be eloquently done by him, being allured rather by the Latin than by the word of God (for at that time I knew not what it meant), I bought it even by the providence of God, as I do now well understand and perceive; and at the first reading (as I well remember) I chanced upon the sentence of St. Paul (O most sweet and comfortable sentence to my soul!) in I Tim. 1, "It is a true saying and worthy of all men to be embraced, that Christ Jesus came into the world to save sinners; of whom I am the chief and principal." This one sentence, through God's instruction and inward working, which I did not then perceive, did so exhilarate my heart, being before wounded with the guilt of my sins, and being almost in despair, that immediately I felt a marvellous comfort and quietness, insomuch "that my bruised bones leaped for joy."[21]

These are the words of Thomas Bilney, one of a group of early English Protestants who met to discuss this new theology at the White Horse Inn at Cambridge in the 1520s. He was burned at the stake in 1531, for reasons we would hardly regard as pivotal today—his opposition to the cult of relics, pilgrimages, and the veneration of saints. But his obedience to the risen Christ impelled him to costly confrontation with ecclesial authority, and we must honor his discipleship no less than his martyrdom. He was one of many who gave their lives so that the privileges of personal faith in Christ and personal reading of the scriptures might be readily available to all—privileges the church now honors universally.

Reforming Agents: (2) The Radical Reformation

There were countless others who shared lesser persecutions as Protestantism wrestled with ecclesial and political freedoms. But always the pattern of their discipleship reflected a radical devotion to spiritual communion with Christ, and a radical commitment to God's compassion and justice in the world. These come together powerfully in our next example, as we turn to what historians describe as the "Radical Reformation"—those persons and movements in which eschatological hope and countercultural life-style challenged church and society alike with God's righteousness, and most especially God's justice for the poor.

The history of these movements includes such well-known names as Thomas Müntzer, Michael Sattler, and Menno Simons.[22] But our example comes from the English Revolution of the mid–seventeenth century: the Diggers, or True Levellers. Led by a layman, Gerrard Winstanley, this radical group sought to establish the right to dig up land enclosed by private owners, in order, as they put it,

> to sow corn and to eat our bread together by the sweat of our brows. And the first reason is this, that we may work in righteousness, and lay the foundation of making the earth a common treasury for all, both rich and poor, that every one that is born in the land may be fed by the earth.[23]

This much is familiar to us from our investigations into the eighth-century prophets and Second-Isaiah.[24] But the Diggers also affirmed the eschatological expectancy of the coming *basileia* of Jesus Christ, as in the following excerpts from *The Diggers' Mirth*, written in 1650:

> The Father he is God alone,
>   nothing besides him is;
> All things are folded in that one,
>   by him all things subsist.
>
> He is our light, our life, our peace,
>   whereby we our being have;
> From him all things have their increase,
>   the tyrant and the slave.
>
> And when the Father seeth it good,
>   and his set time is come;
> He takes away the tyrant's food,
>   and gives it to the Son.
>   · · · · ·
> For there must rise a root of *Jess*,
>   a righteous branch indeed;
> Who setteth free him that's oprest
>   and *Esau* down must tread.
>   · · · · ·

> And thou that as a Lord hast Raign'd
> 　over God's Heritage;
> Thy part thou hast already play'd,
> 　therefore come off the stage.
> 　　　. . . . .
> The time, I say, it is now come,
> 　in which the Lord will make
> All Tyrants servants to the Son,
> 　and he the power will take.
> 　　　. . . . .
> For there shall rise a mighty Stone,
> 　which without hands is cut;
> Which shall the Kingly powers break
> 　he shall be free from shot.
>
> The first that which this Stone shall smite,
> 　shall be the head of Gold;
> A mortal wound he shall them give
> 　now minde thou hast been told.[25]

Gerrard Winstanley has been described as "the culmination of the rhetorical magnificence and ethical seriousness at the heart of the English Revolution."[26] He was certainly in good company, as John Milton, John Lilburne, and others gave eloquent expression to what many regarded as a breaking in of the reign of God, with the abolition of the monarchy and the establishment of a Puritan Commonwealth. This was not to last, however, for in 1660 the monarchy was restored, and the Church of England was reestablished with a punitive code of ecclesiastical legislation. There followed almost thirty years of what Gerald Cragg has termed the "Great Persecution" of the Puritans;[27] and, contrary to the hopes expressed in their poem, it was the radical proposal of the Diggers that faded into the eschatological wings of the social and religious stage. As so often has happened with such *kairos,* the divine *chronos* pronounced the "not yet" of history, and called the servants of God to yet more faithful waiting.

There are those who would identify such movements as utopian, or even communistic, rather than radically Christian. Yet their role as reforming influences in the church and in society at large is extensive, as research into their history increasingly reveals.[28] Moreover, not only is their pedigree unmistakably rooted in the prophecies of the Old Testament; almost single-handedly they have kept alive the eschatological expectancy of the Christian tradition. And the issue they raise for our study, which we shall presently examine in more detail, is how such radical discipleship contributes to the coming reign of God. For one thing is clear: These movements have rarely, if ever, been assimilated into the mainstream of the church.

Reforming Agents: (3) Ecclesiolae in Ecclesia

It is this very issue which is at the heart of our next example, the emergence of small groups within Protestantism as a means of mutual support for a more intentional discipleship. They have become generally known as *ecclesiolae in ecclesia* (little churches in the big church), a phrase that is usually attributed to German pietism of the late seventeenth century, and in particular the *collegia pietatis* (pious groups) of Philipp Jakob Spener, a pastor in the city of Frankfurt.

Spener first opened his home in 1670 for these private meetings, or conventicles, at the request of a number of his parishioners who sought to "confer with one another in simplicity and love," and the format soon spread to other German cities. There was even a *collegium* for the theology students at Tübingen University approved by the faculty in 1677.[29] Religious societies were formed in England along the same lines, and were to provide the basis for John Wesley's Methodist societies a generation later in the eighteenth century.

A Balanced Discipleship

There is a tendency among some historians to regard these pious groups as other-worldly, and ultimately a malleable instrument of secular and religious resistance to social change.[30] Although this is arguably the case in their later years, nothing could be farther from the truth in assessing the impact of the *ecclesiolae* in their prime. Not only did their members make a radical commitment to Christ in their practice of spiritual disciplines, but they also proceeded to live Christ-centered lives. Practical good works were integral to their disciplined discipleship no less than their devotions, as is illustrated by the following excerpt from the *General Rules* of the United [Methodist] Societies, first published in 1743:

> That it may the more easily be discerned whether [the members] are indeed working out their own salvation, each Society is divided into

smaller companies, called Classes, according to their respective places of abode. There are about twelve persons in every class, one of whom is styled *the Leader*. It is his business: . . . To see each person in his class once a week at the least; in order To receive what they are willing to give toward the relief of the poor; To enquire how their souls prosper; To advise, reprove, comfort, or exhort, as occasion may require. . . .

. . . It is therefore expected of all who continue [in these societies] that they should continue to evidence their desire of salvation,

First, By doing no harm, by avoiding evil in every kind—especially that which is most generally practised. . . .

Secondly, By doing good . . . of every possible sort and as far as is possible to all . . .

To their bodies . . . by giving food to the hungry, by clothing the naked, by visiting or helping them that are sick, or in prison. To their souls, by instructing, *reproving*, or exhorting all we have any intercourse with; trampling under foot that enthusiastic doctrine of devils, that "we are not to do good unless *our heart be free to it.*". . .

Thirdly, By attending upon all the ordinances of God. Such are:

The public worship of God;

The ministry of the Word, either read or expounded;

The Supper of the Lord;

. . . private prayer;

Searching the Scriptures; and

Fasting, or abstinence.[31]

The balance here is very clear between the inward spiritual walk with Christ and the outward responsibilities of Christian living in the world, as it was clear in virtually all the various *ecclesiolae* of Protestant piety. Wesley referred to their basics of discipleship as "works of mercy" and "works of piety," and regarded the stipulated weekly class meetings as the "sinews" of his societies, where a healthy tension could be maintained in an environment of mutual accountability.[32] By "watching over each other in love," the members kept close to Christ in word and deed—and thus quickly acquired their nickname, "Methodists."

Staying in the Church

The other mark of these *ecclesiolae* movements was that their leaders, many of whom were ordained clergy, made every endeavor to keep them in the larger church—*in ecclesia*. It was felt that unnecessary separation from the parent body was self-defeating. Not only did it limit their reforming influences; it also distracted from the task of the groups, which was to foster personal piety and practical good works.

Within an ecclesial structure, where doctrines and ordinances were in place, there was freedom to pursue such goals. But once separation occurred, those larger issues had to be addressed all over again. And, as John Wesley observed in his sermon "On Schism," they were usually addressed in a less balanced way than by the larger church, and without due reference to the earliest Christian traditions.[33] To these leaders, the principle seemed to be quite self-evident: An *ecclesiola* that rejects its *ecclesia* must perforce provide its own.

Even so, the reforming influences of the *ecclesiolae* occasioned social and ecclesial opposition, and in some instances this led to separation from the church. Spener found it necessary to publish two pamphlets in 1677, refuting criticism leveled at his *collegia pietatis*,[34] and the religious societies in England had to tread a careful path to avoid ecclesial censure.[35] Moreover, when John Wesley took his evangelistic preaching into the open air, and went so far as to recruit lay helpers and assistants, the opposition he met with was vicious. The record of persecutions in Thomas Jackson's *Lives of Early Methodist Preachers* is all the more eloquent because these dedicated disciples regarded such treatment as quite unexceptional, and to be expected in their line of work.[36] Indeed, the Church of England was ultimately unable to accept the Methodists as reformers. In 1784 they became a separate church in North America, and subsequently throughout the world.

Relating to the Church

It is this which brings us to the pivotal issue of discipleship and ecclesial identity. The question is not the authenticity of these *collegia pietatis* and similar pious groups, nor yet the role of radical Christian movements such as the Diggers in preparing for the reign of God in the world. The small sampling we have taken from the past four hundred years evinces precisely the qualities of discipleship we noted in the earliest days of the church: a directness of relationship with the risen Christ in answer to his call, and a vital concern for the coming of God's *shalom* in the world. Further investigations would merely confirm the sampling.

When it is Christ-centered, radical piety has time and again been at the forefront of social reform, as Donald Dayton convincingly illustrates in his classic study of the nineteenth-century evangelical heritage.[37] And likewise when it is Christ-centered, radical justice has proved to be rooted in spiritual disciplines, as the Anti-Slavery and Civil Rights movements in the United States have powerfully demonstrated.[38] The impact of authentic Christian discipleship on the world is incontrovertible and self-evident.

The question which rather concerns us is how this kind of discipleship relates to the institutional church. For throughout the history of Christianity, the first question faced by faithful disciples when they have found themselves forming groups or movements has almost always been that of separation. The Roman Catholic Church has dealt with this most creatively in the formation of religious orders, many of which are with us to this day. But when Protestantism broke from Rome, the question of reform within the church inevitably raised the possibility of forming yet more new churches. And in the North American church, denominational diversity has in fact been the norm.

The question is by no means one of academic history. It is faced by local church pastors in the United States week by week, and it is pivotal to our study. For if disciplined Christian disciples are to have a recognized place in the church and a healthy and positive relationship with their fellow members, including the pastor and the ecclesial hierarchy, then their identity in the congregation must be established no less than that of the congregation in the world. If this cannot be done, their reforming example is destined time and again to lose its influence in the church; and by the same token, their influence in society will lose the particular impact which comes from rootage in the Christian tradition.

A Modern Case Study: Base Ecclesial Communities

It is no accident that these are the very questions being faced by one of the most dramatic and effective Roman Catholic church renewal movements in this half of the century, the *comunidades eclesiais de base* (base ecclesial communities) of Latin America. If the time of their birthing could be identified, then it would probably be the Second General Conference of the Latin American Bishops at Medellin, Colombia, in 1968. But establishing such a date would be altogether moot; for, as Guillermo Cook makes clear in his definitive history, *The Expectation of the Poor*, the CEBs are a renewal from the underside of history. "Socio-politically, the Catholic *comunidades* are the most notable evidence in Christendom today of the poor demanding their place in the sun."[39]

In this regard, we should note that the word "base" does not mean devotion to the basics of Christian faith or social reform, but rather that these communities are formed at the base of human society—the grassroots. With or without the cooperation of their local parish church, they ground their life and work in a constant process of communal action and reflection: living and working as disciples in the world; praying and reflecting on the scriptures to give meaning to their existence.

Prior to Medellin, there was the *Movimento de Educação de Base* in Northeastern Brazil, dating back to 1956; and it is significant that the dynamic of this was lay catechesis. The tradition is that an old woman in Natal asked her bishop during a pastoral visit why their church had to stay dark when a neighboring church was lit each evening. "Because there is no priest," was the reply. To which she asked in return, "Does everything have to stop simply because we have no priest?"[40] From this seed, leadership of the movement quickly passed to the local grassroots of the community; but it was only after Medellin that there was ecclesial openness to this expression of discipleship, and the adoption of the pedagogy of Paulo Freire, whose principle of *conscientization,* or consciousness-raising, has become the watchword of the movement.

Base communities in general have three orientations: a reappropriation of the Bible as the book of all the people in the community of faith; an awareness of their socioeconomic context and the word of biblical justice which challenges this reality; and a desire to reform the ecclesial structure, especially what they regard as the outmoded model of the parish church.[41] Thus it is not surprising to find that the *comunidades* have been controversial within the church, and have been actively persecuted by many governments, at times to the point where they have had to go underground. Even so, they have become widespread in Latin America, and in many other countries throughout the world.

Not that their growth has been an unqualified success story. Many have failed, leadership has increasingly proved to be a problem, and some have become politically or religiously sectarian. But there is no question that as a movement they are a sign of God's righteousness and justice in the world. In Brazil, where they were first to be reckoned with as a force, there were 40,000 CEBs by 1974; 80,000 by 1979; and more recently, an estimated 100,000, with another 80,000 throughout the rest of Latin America.[42]

The reason for this proliferation, suggests Cook, is their self-understanding. Their referent is the *koinonia* of the early church, the house *ekklēsia*; and in this *koinonia* there is a hermeneutic of what Juan Luis Segundo has described as "ideological suspicion."[43] What does the Bible really have to say about the human condition, socially as well as personally? Why did Jesus command the disciples to meet together? And if a hermeneutic of communal insight implies that Christ and Christ alone is to be obeyed, how do we discern the will of Christ?

There is much about this movement which is highly reminiscent of the examples we have just cited from the Protestant reforming traditions: the discovery of the Bible as a source of Christian living in the world; the exhilaration of finding that ecclesial hierarchies are resistible; the deep inward assurance of a personal relationship with Christ, which comes from shared discipleship; the commitment to radical justice in the world, which inevitably follows from such a relationship; and the tendency to become religiously and politically sectarian when rejected by the church.

Perhaps most significant, however, and equally reminiscent of the Reformation, is that the *comunidades* are now evincing a highly distinctive spirituality. Initially this was slow to develop. Their struggle for social justice dominated much of their early agenda, and their relations with the ecclesial hierarchy were abrasive as they sought to establish an identity. But in recent years, there has emerged what Gustavo Gutiérrez has described as a spirituality of liberation:

> Encounter with the Lord is the point of departure for a life according to the Spirit. This life finds expression in a journey in search of God . . . what Paul calls "a more excellent way" . . . [But] we are talking here about the journey of an entire people and not of isolated individuals. The paradigmatic experience of the Jewish people in its exodus . . . the way by which the Spirit leads the new "messianic people" the church, through history . . . a journey which is a collective one because an entire community accomplishes it.[44]

Leonardo Boff has gone so far as to describe these base communities as an *ecclesiogenesis*, a rebirth of the church, patterned on the early *ekklēsia*.[45] Yet he is careful to make clear that this does not mean a replacement of the existing church. He regards the episcopate, the priesthood, and other features of the ecclesial structure as permanent and basic. They provide "union, universality, and bonding with the great witnesses of the apostolic past."[46]

The question he raises for the Roman Catholic hierarchy is how these ecclesial offices relate to the body of the church. Do they function over it, or within it? Do they respect the various charisms of the grassroots communities of the church? For it is this latter style which "translates the gospel attitude, and is the praxis that Jesus willed for the Messianic community."[47]

Familiar Questions

The questions are familiar. They have been posed by every *kairos* reforming movement since ecclesial structures evolved in the *chronos* of God's salvation. They come to us with particular cogency from the *comunidades de base*, however, since the *comunidades* happen to be a significant movement in today's world church. Moreover they are questions our North American *ecclesia* needs to ask about its own *ecclesiolae*, and its more radical reforming movements.[48]

It is not that such groups and movements need to be fostered: The Holy Spirit calls them into being with predictable unpredictability. They continue to comprise dedicated disciples, whose concern is to pattern their lives after Jesus of Nazareth and to work with the risen Christ in preparing for the coming reign of God. To the extent that the larger church accepts them, they work within congregations to provide leadership and renewal. To the extent that they are rejected, they move out from the church to minister directly to the world. To the extent that they are alienated, they become radically sectarian, even to the point of losing their churchly identity. All of these possibilities are apparent from their history throughout two millennia, and apparent to us today. Yet time and again, God affirms them at the cutting edge of the coming *basileia*. They are a permanent phenomenon of the church: They are Christ's authentic disciples.

Keeping the Blockage Clear

What we must seek, therefore, if our ecclesial channels are to remain unblocked, is the incorporation of such disciples into a shared leadership of the church, where they can be regarded not as eccentric or radical or marginal, but as an integral and permanent part of the ecclesial hierarchy. This is not a recommendation for mere social wisdom—allowing spontaneous community and social structure to interplay creatively.[49] It is rather the most critical of ecclesiological questions—whether the church might be more genuinely and energetically under the headship of Christ if those who count the cost and make the commitment to a disciplined discipleship, as did the members of the primitive Christian house *ekklēsia*, were to join the ordained clergy, not as subordinates, but as necessary colleagues in the pastoral leadership of congregations.

It is the word *necessary* that must now occupy us in the conclusion of our investigation. For if God's saving grace is universally at work in the world, as we have argued from scripture; and if the church is a particular means of that grace, heralding the Christ whose *parousia* will make the reign of God truly universal; and if there are those who, in every generation of humankind, are called by God to the particular task of a disciplined obedience to Jesus Christ; then we cannot leave all of this on the ecclesiological drawing board. We must ask how it translates into our own particular ecclesial setting—the average North American congregation. And if it fits, then we must do something about it.

CHRIST-CENTERED CONGREGATIONS

Ekklēsia in Ecclesia

Once we have cleared our blockage of grace in the life and work of the church, the formula is really very simple. We must permit those persons in our congregations who are the successors to the early house *ekklēsia* of the church to function as leaders in the *ecclesia*, the larger church of institutional Christianity. The former are called by Christ to be disciplined disciples. The latter, as the community of faith, are no less called by Christ to proclaim and witness to the Good News of God's salvation. If Christ is not to be divided, these two parts of the body must function together in the world, where the Holy Spirit is universally at work, preparing for the coming reign of God.

Necessary Distinctions

To accept such a formula means reminding ourselves of some of the distinctions we have drawn throughout our study. But before we do, we must be clear that the word "distinction" does not imply "separation." It is helpful in this regard to take Paul's analogy of the body, in which he places the different parts under the headship of Christ (Rom. 12; I Cor. 12). The limbs and organs are distinct because they have different functions to perform. Yet they belong to the same body. If one part hurts, the whole body hurts; if one part rejoices, then all rejoice.

136

(1) *Church and World*

With this understanding of "distinction," we can be reminded first that the church is distinct from the rest of the world, yet very much a part of it. Salvation is not the distinguishing factor here, because Christ has died for all. Not everyone has accepted this gift of salvation as yet, but God's grace will persevere into all eternity, as will God's judgment, until Christ's long, slow victory has come to fulfillment. God does not foreclose: Salvation is for all.

The distinction of the church in the world is rather that of election—election for a purpose. And the purpose is to be God's messengers of Good News to a world which is lost, but is being found; which is blind, but is being made to see; which is captive, but is being liberated; which is sick, but is being healed. This *evangel*, this Good News of salvation, is to be proclaimed to everyone as the announcement of what God has done in Jesus Christ. Our salvation is accomplished, and it will come to fulfillment with the coming of a new age, a new order, in which universal love, justice, and peace will prevail on earth as in heaven, to all eternity.

The invitation which comes with this message is simple and direct: Accept it. Accept this salvation. It is the birthright of all humanity, and it requires only our surrender to its gracious reality.

(2) Kairos *and* Chronos

The *kairos* of this message, the critical "day of the Lord," is that now is the time of salvation. Now is the time to accept God's gracious initiative. Now is the time of forgiveness and reconciliation. Now is the time to repent and be converted back to God. But the *chronos* of God's salvation is also a distinctive reality. The eschatological clock is still running. History is still unfolding. And in spite of much progress and much labor, the reign of God is not yet here in its fullness. We still await the *parousia* of Jesus Christ, when time and eternity will be fused in a glorious and ultimate resurrection.

(3) *Salvation and Discipleship*

Because this echatological clock is still running, the third and crucial distinction in removing our blockage of grace is to acknowledge that discipleship and salvation are not the same thing. Not every Christian is called to be a disciple in the sense of the word we find in scripture. We have discussed the reasons for this in some detail, but the key factor lies in what John Wesley termed "degrees of faith." People respond to the gospel in different ways and at different times. If we invert the gospel into an anthropocentric message, making our salvation in Christ the variable and human response the constant, then we usurp the divine prerogative of judgment on other human beings, and presume to pronounce on who does and does not have faith. It is rather our salvation in Christ that is the constant, and human response the variable; which means that we must accept a very wide range of Christian commitment in our congregations.

Indeed, this is precisely what we do accept, every Sunday morning. We welcome them all, from the casual enquirer, to the earnest seeker, to the habitual hanger-on, to the seasoned resister, to the faithful worker, to the unassuming saint. And the gospel of light and salt and leaven and seed (Matt. 5:13-16; Luke 13:18-33), is that in and through Jesus Christ, crucified, risen, and soon to come again, this very mixed community called church is as justified by grace as every one of its members; as also is the world, the larger family of prodigals, whose return God awaits with infinite patience and longing.

The Ministry of Jesus

When we turn to the New Testament, we find the same distinctions in the ministry of Jesus. On the one hand, he had many followers. Without any hint of irony or resentment, he called them his flock, because they needed a shepherd to guide and enfold them (Matt. 9:36, 10:6; Mark 6:34; John 10:1ff., 21:15ff.). When they were stranded in the desert without food, he fed them (Matt. 14:15-21). And by letting us know that the essential nature of God is parental, he made clear that the flock was one large family, and that God wants them all back home where they belong (Luke 15:11-32).

Yet the call of Jesus to discipleship, as we have also inferred from the scriptures, was direct and demanding (Luke 14:25-33). Not only did Jesus expect his disciples to share his confrontation with the forces of Beelzebul. When he described himself as the good shepherd (John 10:11, 14), he clearly expected them to assist him with the pastoral task of tending his larger flock. When he fed the multitude of followers in the desert, it was the disciples who distributed the bread and the fish

(Matt. 14:19; Mark 6:41; Luke 9:16); and after his resurrection, it was his direct and threefold instruction to Peter to feed his sheep (John 21:15-17).

This has been the pattern across two thousand years of Christian history. The whole world, by prevenient grace, hears the call of God. Whether or not they are Christian, they yearn for the bread of life; they are hungry for spiritual food. They must be fed no less readily than the thousands to whom Jesus handed out the loaves and fishes. The high privilege of those of us who call ourselves Christian is the particular grace of telling the world that salvation is indeed a present and future reality in the Jew of Nazareth, Jesus the Christ, and that everyone belongs to God's family.

In a well-Christianized country such as the United States, many of this larger family find their way into the particular family of the church. They come to worship, often with marked regularity. Many of them endeavor to follow Christ, believing his teachings, and obeying his commandments. Not infrequently, they honor him at great personal cost. For all these reasons, they value the fellowship of the church family. This is where they are nurtured by the manifold grace of word, sacrament, and community. And in turn, they share this grace with the world, witnessing to Christ in word and deed, and imparting many of the firstfruits of the reign of God.

By the same token, however, the call to discipleship is as direct and demanding today as it was for those whom Jesus first called. Not only must the disciples of Jesus Christ reach out to the larger family of Christ in the world. They must also help to feed the particular community called church, so that Christians as a body can minister to the whole of humankind with grace and power. And if a priority can be inferred from the training of the twelve, it would be the nurturing of this particular body for its mission to the world. For not even Jesus tried to go it alone. One of the first acts of his ministry was to select this group of followers, who subsequently became his friends. From what we can tell, they were not especially gifted; nor did they seem to be particularly quick on the uptake. But they did have one outstanding distinguishing characteristic: their readiness to follow Jesus in answer to his call.

This call to discipleship has always been difficult to accept; and even if accepted, difficult to comprehend. It requires the discipline of commitment, yet it rarely brings recognition, even less, prestige. The first disciples came to understand their role slowly, and at times agonizingly. But eventually they came to see that Jesus had not chosen them for a special status. Rather, he wanted them for a special task (Matt. 20:1-16; Mark 10:28-31; Luke 13:22-30). Their relationship with Christ was for a purpose: to nurture the immediate family, and thereby all the world (Mark 9:33-35).

To understand the nature of Christian discipleship today, we must accept all of these distinctions anew. There is the family of God, the people of God throughout the world, who need to be taught, healed, fed, and loved. Then there are those who belong to the community called church, the particular channel of grace through which the gospel can provide teaching and healing and feeding, so that God's love, justice, and peace, already present in the world, may be known and honored by all the world. And then there are those who are called to a disciplined Christian discipleship, whose task it is to lead the community called church in its ministry and mission, and to ensure that it is indeed a Christ-Centered means of grace for the world.

A Wide Range of Ministry

The perimeters of our study require us to leave aside the implications of these distinctions for our global ministry and mission, which are considerable, and ask what is the significance of accepting them within the spectrum of our North American congregational life.

First, it means that our churchly identity must be one of an inclusive, unconditional, open, gracious community. Congregations must be places where people find forgiveness and reconciliation in Christ through the infinitely varied and empathetic working of the Holy Spirit, irrespective of their response to the gospel or the depth of their commitment to Christian discipleship. For this we need a very wide range of pastoral ministries, which require us to be not only in mission to the world, but also in ministry to one another. Thus we must not only announce and witness to the Good News of God's salvation in the world, but we must also build up the church in a communion of God's love. Our ministries of service, worship, teaching, and healing must nurture our members as well as pointing to the coming of God's new order of justice—the fulfillment of God's reign of love on earth as in heaven.

A Practical Example

To see what this means in practical terms, we can take as an illustration the servant and prophetic ministries of the church—*diakonia* and *kerygma*. Where they are sensitively planned and implemented, taking into account the breadth of commitment in a congregation, these two ministries can function in creative complementarity. In this way, the church can truly be a sign community of salt, light, leaven, and seed in the world, and a prophetic messenger of God's justice.

There are persons in our congregations who will be ready to assist with the practical ministries of neighborly service, either locally or globally; and there are those who will commit to leadership in this field, ensuring that these ministries are not undertaken irresponsibly. Likewise, there are those who will support and affirm prophetic stands on social justice; and there are those who will emerge as leaders in these areas, ready to confront the powers and principalities of the present world order in the name of Jesus Christ.

The complementarity of these ministries lies in the fact that many who serve their neighbor with compassion may not be ready for the political implications of proclaiming God's justice. By the same token, many who stand for justice may lack the patience to minister compassionately to those in need. If we accept the reality of "degrees" of faith response to the gospel, however, then all of these dimensions—compassionate service, prophetic pronouncement of God's justice, those who lead, and those who follow or affirm—all can work together for the advancement of the reign of God.

By contrast, a failure to work with differing degrees of commitment can lead to the impairment of these ministries; which regrettably is all too common in our present North American ecclesial life. Take, for example, the proclamation of God's justice. An unwillingness to accept and nurture prophetic ministry in many local congregations, which at first is likely to be tentative or even timid as people explore these potentially confrontative channels of grace, has led to these issues being shouldered almost exclusively by national agencies or caucuses. This has resulted in a twofold handicap. On the one hand, congregations feel largely relieved of their responsibilities in this area. They tend therefore to focus their social outreach on neighborly acts of compassion, as often as not dealing with the symptoms of injustice to the neglect of its causes; whereas both dimensions are vitally important, and scriptural. On the other hand, denominational and ecumenical agencies or caucuses are often left to forge prophetic ministry for the church without the support, and more important without the guidance, of local congregations, whose common sense is often the best sensor of how to communicate with and influence the world in which we live.

Centered on Christ Jesus

The same inferences can be drawn for other dimensions of the life and work of the church. Once the center of congregational life is the risen Christ, then the richness and diversity of ministry is limitless—as we observed when we examined the implications of a Christ-Centered evangelism.[1] With all of our faith, works, gifts, and resources focused on Christ Jesus, our ecclesial communities can truly be particular means of grace. And this grace, combining with the grace of the Holy Spirit universally at work in the world, will hold the church in faithful servanthood, actively expecting the fullness of God's *shalom*.

Without a Christ-Centeredness, however, it is unlikely that congregations will be sensitive to these differing modes of participation and depths of commitment among their members. And this in turn will foster a lack of sensitivity to the needs of the community at large—ironically, the surest indication of an anthropocentric mindset in a congregation. As Ezra Earl Jones has cogently argued, the primary task of congregations is to focus on the wider human community as God's sphere of saving activity. We are to accept people where they are, relate them to God, and empower them for ministry and mission to the world.[2] Congregations not centered on Christ, however, tend to become self-centered—so concerned about the health and vitality of the church that instead of being channels of grace to the world they expend most of their energies on themselves. And this, as we have argued, is precisely what constitutes our present North American ecclesial blockage.

The question we must finally address, therefore, is what might happen in a congregation in the event that this blockage is cleared. Suppose we do identify our anthropocentrism, and revert to a theocentrism. Suppose that, instead of being ecclesial safe-houses, mired in centripetal inertia, we become centrifugal channels of grace for the world. Suppose we become so Christ-Centered that people are drawn to wellsprings of grace, to be fed and healed and taught and loved, just as they were drawn to Jesus of Nazareth. Suppose we do become authentic sign communities, which so influence our cultural environment with the *evangel* of God's love, peace, and justice, that large numbers of people join our ranks to work for God's *shalom*. Suppose that all this were to happen. How then would we facilitate such congregational ministry and mission? How would we keep it Christ-Centered? Most directly of all, How could we begin such a process here and now in local congregations, without waiting for the whole of the church to be reformed and recentered on Christ?

The Challenge of Radical Discipleship

At this point we must once again be reminded that the focus of our study is the United States of America, where the church has for several centuries been an integral part of the culture. As a result, and as we have noted, the larger *ecclesia*, the institutional church, reflects a great deal of its cultural surroundings, and by no means always manifests the costly discipleship which marked the early Christian *ekklēsia*. For those who make a commitment to such costly discipleship, therefore, the recurring question is whether and how this larger institutional church can be regarded as the church at all.

As we have also noted, the question is by no means an academic one; nor is it new. Those who seek to follow Jesus Christ faithfully in the world are often restless in the larger North American *ecclesia*. They seek a more radical discipleship, one that goes back to the roots of the early *ekklēsia*, to primitive Christian commitment. And so they align themselves with movements of spiritual renewal such as *Cursillo* or *Walk to Emmaus*—the modern *ecclesiolae*; they form caucuses for more radical social action within their denominations, or seek more direct involvement in organizations like *Amnesty International* or *Witness for Peace*—the "Diggers" and "True Levellers" of the late twentieth century; and there are those who, like the *comunidades de base* of Latin America, form intentional Christian communities at the grassroots of society, such as *Sojourners* in Washington, D.C., or *Jubilee* in Philadelphia, Pennsylvania.[3]

And yet, while all of these expressions of a more radical piety and a more radical justice in the world are significant contributions to the coming reign of God, there remains the issue of the institutional *ecclesia*. For in spite of repeated affirmations and protestations from these radical disciples that they are *in ecclesia*, it is difficult to avoid the inference that in many instances they have distanced themselves from what they perceive to be a large, enculturated, compromised, or even apostate church. And to the extent that their witness is incisive, it presents countless pastoral leaders of the *ecclesia* with the unresolved dilemma we laid out in chapter 1 of this study: How does one lead with integrity in a congregation where costly discipleship is not a prerequisite of membership? How does one establish Christ-Centered priorities when most of the pastoral workload comprises the feeding of a flock that seems to have an insatiable appetite for spiritual junk food, and which is by no means immune to spiritual amphetamines?

A Justified Ecclesia

The answer lies in yet another question: What should we realistically expect from a church that has entered into the bloodstream of a culture? Once we pose this question, it comes as something of a surprise to realize that in point of fact it is very rarely addressed, and for a reason likewise rarely taken into account: that the church has been in existence for the better part of two thousand years. This means that Christianity has a considerable track record, much of it mixed; and moreover, has experienced the blessing, also mixed, of being thoroughly institutionalized for much of that time. The challenge of radical discipleship, therefore, is that it inevitably exposes the drawbacks of such a history: the compromises, the enculturations, and the frequent surrender of God's *kairos* and *chronos* alike to the powers and principalities of this world.

There is another perspective, however, which we need keep in view, namely the immense potential of a large *in*culturated church, extensively implanted in a nation's social fabric, for the raising of people's consciousness and expectation of the coming reign of God. What might happen in such an ecclesial setting if, to borrow Ernst Bloch's dramatic imagery, time were to invade the cathedral, and impel such an *ecclesia* to a radical expectation of *shalom?*[4]

Clearly such a church would have to hold itself under the *kairos* of God's righteousness and justice, and always give the kerygmatic gospel a ready hearing. The prophetic word of God would never have to be patronized as eccentric (in which case it can always be ignored) nor yet branded as disruptive (in which case it can always be silenced). The bias of God toward the poor and the helpless would have to be the watchword of this *ecclesia* for all the world to see and take heed.

By the same token, such a church would have to be accountable to the *chronos* of Christ's "long, slow victory." It would have to acknowledge that growth toward *shalom* is a divine initiative no less than the *novum* of its final coming. While accepting that the *parousia* remains a mystery, the task of preparing for this final victory of Christ would have to be as vigorous as if it were to be scheduled for tomorrow. It would be the clear, God-given responsibility of such a church to be in an attitude of active expectancy, faithful hope, and constant service.

Can we realistically expect all of this from a large, enculturated church? God's universal grace gives us only one possible answer: an unequivocal affirmative. The *ecclesia* is justified by grace no less than its individual members. The institutional church, radical Christian discipleship, and everything in between, are all acceptable to God through the merits of Christ, and are therefore usable by God in the long, slow work of salvation.

Leaders in Discipleship

All of this is contingent, however, on the critical necessity for Christ-Centered congregations. Everything we have said about the *ecclesia* as a sign community, as a witnessing, serving, proclaiming, healing, worshiping, praying, prophetic community of love, justice, and peace, can be accomplished only by grace. The visible church must be a sacrament of God's salvation in Christ Jesus, and the parts of its body must be seen to conform to the inaugurated *basileia tou theou.*

If this is to be true of local congregations, then our immediate task is very clear indeed. We need to make room for disciplined disciples to share the leadership of the church, who will keep the church centered on Jesus Christ. Such leaders cannot be trained, still less equipped. They can only be *developed.* This leadership must come from those who are willing to role-model authentic Christian discipleship by making a disciplined commitment to the will of Christ Jesus; whose driving concern is a consistent walk with God.[5] Such persons will not be *ecclesiolae* so much as the new *ekklēsia*, the company of those who have accepted the cost of discipleship, who expect the Holy Spirit to be in their midst when they gather in the name of Christ—the hermeneutic of *koinonia* which marked the primitive Christian community.[6]

Though they are few and far between today, there once was a time when our congregations were rich in such mentors. Many of us can remember them from our childhood and youth. They grounded us in the faith, and showed us the way to live it out in the world: the Sunday school teachers who taught us all year from one book, which most of the time they did not need; the mothers and fathers of the church who could tell us with authority what it meant to be obedient to Jesus Christ in all things; the saints who kept their appointments with God, and thus knew God, and hungered and thirsted for righteousness; the prophets who thundered God's justice in high places—and especially the high places close to home in our communities, towns, and cities.

Such mentors will be needed again if our ecclesial channels of grace become unblocked. They will be needed to lead us in worship and devotion, in compassion and justice. They will be needed to tradition the gospel within the church, and to show us how to tradition it for the world. They will be needed to keep alive the hope of the coming reign of God, on earth as in heaven, and to show us how to live in that *basileia* here and now as a foretaste of God's love, justice, and peace.

We will find them again, however, only if we allow them to become our mentors, and let them share in the leadership of congregations. They must be acknowledged, commissioned, respected, and affirmed in their disciplined commitment: not as those who are privileged, but as those who are responsible; not as those who are closer to Christ than the rest of us, but as those who are more seasoned in their obedience to Christ; not as those who, already saved, are showing the rest of us how to be saved, but as those who, treading the path ahead, are showing the rest of us how to work out our salvation.

Such leaders in discipleship are present in our congregations. If we will recognize them for who they are, welcome them as mentors, and affirm their disciplined commitment, our churchly agenda will increasingly focus on Jesus Christ, not only in our ministries of word and sacrament, but also in the very fiber of our worldly living. There need be no hesitancy in taking such a step, no need to hold back such leaders for fear that a virtuoso religiousness might inhibit the less committed of our members. For with our salvation sure in Christ Jesus, and grace lavished on all creation, the call to discipleship can be answered in complete freedom. Knowing that God does not foreclose on anyone or anything, we can recognize Christ's latest disciples for who they are: the *ekklēsia* of God, leading God's church and the whole of God's people toward Christ's final victory.

N O T E S

INTRODUCTION
A MAJOR ECCLESIAL BLOCKAGE

1. See "Questions of Context" (below, p. 15) where this use of "North American" is explained.
2. Alfred Loisy, *The Gospel and the Church* (New York: Charles Scribner's Sons, 1912), p. 166.
3. See Charles H. Kraft, *Christianity in Culture: A Study in Dynamic Biblical Theologizing in Cross-Cultural Perspective* (Maryknoll, N.Y.: Orbis Books, 1979), p. 318.
4. Jürgen Moltmann, *The Church in the Power of the Spirit* (New York: Harper & Row, 1977).
5. Frederick Herzog, *Justice Church: The New Function of the Church in North American Christianity* (Maryknoll, N.Y.: Orbis Books, 1980).
6. Howard A. Snyder, *Signs of the Spirit: How God Reshapes the Church* (Grand Rapids, Mich.: Zondervan Academie Books, 1989).
7. Leonardo Boff, *Ecclesiogenesis: The Base Communities Reinvent the Church* (Maryknoll, N.Y.: Orbis Books, 1986).
8. Jacques Ellul, *The Presence of the Kingdom* (New York: Seabury Press, 1967), pp. 61ff. (French ed., 1948).
9. See, for example, Donald A. McGavran, *Effective Evangelism: A Theological Mandate* (Phillipsburg, N.J.: Presbyterian and Reformed Publishing Company, 1988). Afterword by Roger S. Greenway, pp. 140f.
10. Carl E. Braaten, *The Flaming Center: A Theology of the Christian Mission* (Philadelphia: Fortress Press, 1977), pp. 115ff.
11. This vivid metaphor emerged during a discussion with Carl Braaten at the Academy for Evangelism in Theological Education, meeting at Candler School of Theology, Emory University, Atlanta, Ga., in October 1987.
12. Stanley Hauerwas and William H. Willimon, *Resident Aliens: Life in the Christian Colony* (Nashville: Abingdon Press, 1989).
13. Ibid., p. 92.
14. See below, pp. 91ff.
15. J. C. Hoekendijk, *The Church Inside Out* (Philadelphia: Westminster Press, 1966).

CHAPTER ONE
THE NORTH AMERICAN DILEMMA

1. See, for example, Urban T. Holmes, *Turning to Christ: A Theology of Renewal and Evangelization* (New York: Seabury Press, 1981), pp. 202ff.

2. Jimmy Carter, "The Task of Evangelism," *Journal of the Academy for Evangelism in Theological Education*, vol. 3 (1987–1988), p. 7.

3. Robert E. Cushman, "Biblical Election as Sacred History," in *Our Common History as Christians: Essays in Honor of Albert C. Outler*, ed. John Deschner, Leroy T. Howe, and Klaus Penzel (New York: Oxford University Press, 1975), p. 210.

4. See James D. Anderson and Ezra Earl Jones, *Ministry of the Laity* (San Francisco: Harper & Row, 1986), pp. 100ff., where the authors argue for the church to reverse this role, and see "as its primary referent the common good of the community in which it is located" (p. 102).

5. David B. Barrett, *Cosmos, Chaos, and Gospel: A Chronology of World Evangelization from Creation to New Creation* (Birmingham, Ala.: New Hope, 1987), p. 75.

6. Orlando E. Costas, *Christ Outside the Gate: Mission Beyond Christendom* (Maryknoll, N.Y.: Orbis Books, 1982), p. 79.

7. Eberhard Bethge, Renate Bethge, and Christian Gremmels, eds., *Dietrich Bonhoeffer: A Life in Pictures* (Philadelphia: Fortress Press, 1986).

8. Ibid., p. 234.

9. Ibid., p. 159.

10. Ibid., p. 180.

11. Mary Craig, *Six Modern Martyrs* (New York: Crossroad Publishing Co., 1985).

12. See, for example, John Wimber, with Kevin Springer, *Power Evangelism* (San Francisco: Harper & Row, 1986), pp. 107ff.

13. Kurt W. Back, *Beyond Words: The Story of Sensitivity Training and the Encounter Movement* (Baltimore, Md.: Penguin Books, 1973), pp. 229ff.

14. Philip J. Lee, *Against the Protestant Gnostics* (New York: Oxford University Press, 1987), p. 228.

15. Alfred C. Krass, *Five Lanterns at Sundown: Evangelism in a Chastened Mood* (Grand Rapids, Mich.: Wm. B. Eerdmans, 1978).

16. Ibid., p. 35.

17. *Religion in America: 50 Years: 1935–1985* (Princeton, N.J.: Gallup Report No. 236, May 1985).

CHAPTER TWO
PARTICULAR VOCATION: CHRISTIAN DISCIPLESHIP

1. John E. Stambaugh and David L. Balch, *The New Testament in Its Social Environment*. Library of Early Christianity, Wayne A. Meeks, general ed. (Philadelphia: Westminster Press, 1986), p. 121.

2. Cf. John 13:16, 15:20.

3. *The Interpreter's Dictionary of the Bible*, 4 vols. (Nashville: Abingdon Press, 1962); *Supplementary Volume* (Abingdon, 1976), 1:845. Many of the scriptural references throughout this chapter are also drawn from here.

4. Michael H. Crosby, *House of Disciples: Church, Economics, and Justice in Matthew* (Maryknoll, N.Y.: Orbis Books, 1988), p. 44.

5. Ibid. See also William R. Farmer, *Jesus and the Gospel* (Philadelphia: Fortress Press, 1982), pp. 63ff.

6. Cf. Mark 1:16-20; Luke 5:1-11.

7. Crosby, *Disciples*, pp. 92f.

8. See also Matt. 13:57, 23:34, 37; Mark 6:4; Luke 4:24.

9. Richard A. Edwards, "Uncertain Faith: Matthew's Portrait of the Disciples," in *Discipleship in the New Testament*, ed. and intro. by Fernando F. Segovia (Philadelphia: Fortress Press, 1985), pp. 57ff.

10. Norman H. Snaith, *The Distinctive Ideas of the Old Testament* (New York: Schocken Books, 1964), pp. 52f.

11. Ibid., pp. 68f.

12. Ibid., p. 69.

13. Ibid., p. 76.

14. Ibid., pp. 86f.

15. This dynamic of necessary forgiveness is given a powerful and innovative exposition by Jacques Ellul in *The Politics of God and the Politics of Man* (Grand Rapids, Mich.: Wm. B. Eerdmans, 1972), pp. 36ff.

16. Frederick Herzog, *Liberation Theology: Liberation in the Light of the Fourth Gospel* (New York: Seabury Press, 1972), p. 175.

17. Ibid., pp. 174ff.

18. Segovia, *Discipleship*, p. 2. See also C. S. C. Williams, *A Commentary on The Acts of the Apostles* (London: Adam & Charles Black, 1957), p. 291.

19. Stambaugh and Balch, *N.T. Social Environment*, p. 52.

20. Ibid., p. 55.

21. Crosby, *Disciples*, pp. 35f., 96f.

22. See, for example, Leon Festinger, "Informal Social Communication," in *Group Dynamics: Research and Theory*, ed. Dorwin Cartwright and Alvin Zander, 3rd ed. (New York: Harper & Row, 1968), pp. 182ff.

23. William J. Abraham, *The Logic of Evangelism* (Grand Rapids, Mich.: Wm. B. Eerdmans, 1989), chps. 5–7.

24. Michael Walsh, *The Triumph of the Meek: Why Early Christianity Succeeded* (San Francisco: Harper & Row, 1986), p. 112.

25. *Interpreter's Dictionary*, 3:660.

26. Geoffrey Wainwright, *Eucharist and Eschatology* (New York: Oxford University Press, 1981), p. 14.

27. See Wayne A. Meeks, *The First Urban Christians: The Social World of the Apostle Paul* (New Haven: Yale University Press, 1983), pp. 94ff.

CHAPTER THREE
UNIVERSAL GRACE: THE COMING REIGN OF GOD

1. Hauerwas and Willimon, *Resident Aliens*, pp. 15ff.

2. Richard John Neuhaus, *Time Toward Home: The American Experiment as Revelation* (New York: Seabury Press, 1975), p. 209.

3. *The Works of John Wesley: Volume 7: A Collection of Hymns for the Use of the People Called Methodists*, ed. Franz Hildebrandt and Oliver A. Beckerlegge, asst.

James Dale (New York: Oxford University Press, 1983. Reprint. Nashville: Abingdon Press), pp. 125f.

4. Mircea Eliade, *The Sacred and the Profane: The Nature of Religion* (New York: Harcourt, Brace & World, 1959), pp. 110f.

5. Gene L. Davenport, *Into the Darkness: Discipleship in the Sermon on the Mount* (Nashville: Abingdon Press, 1988), pp. 225f.

6. Jürgen Moltmann, *Theology of Hope: On the Ground and the Implications of a Christian Eschatology* (New York: Harper & Row, 1967), p. 34.

7. Frederick W. Danker, *Jesus and the New Age: A Commentary on the Third Gospel* (St. Louis, Mo.: Clayton Publishing House, 1972), p. 181.

8. "Luke never views the Kingdom of God as a psychological reality. It is always God's reigning action" (Danker, *New Age*, p. 181). See also Justo González, *Christian Thought Revisited: Three Types of Theology* (Nashville: Abingdon Press, 1989), for an illuminating examination of Christian theological origins. González argues that there have been three types of theology throughout the history of the church, each traceable to a particular geographic area in primitive Christianity. Using Tertullian as an exemplar of Type A, with Law as its main thrust, and Origen for Type B, with Truth as its main thrust, González selects Irenaeus to exemplify Type C, with History as its main thrust—but history "in the sense that all that takes place within time is guided toward God's future." What is noteworthy about this is that "Irenaeus' theology was eminently pastoral. He himself was a pastor, and his writings had pastoral purposes. But even further, Irenaeus saw God as the great Shepherd who leads the flock toward the divine purposes" (p. 31). González regards the rediscovery of this Type C as a highly significant development in twentieth-century theology (p. 140).

9. M. Douglas Meeks, *God the Economist: The Doctrine of God and Political Economy* (Minneapolis: Fortress Press, 1989), p. 120. See also Crosby, *Disciples*, p. 211.

10. Meeks, *God the Economist*, p. 34. See also pp. 95ff.

11. Mortimer Arias, *Announcing the Reign of God: Evangelization and the Subversive Memory of Jesus* (Philadelphia: Fortress Press, 1984), pp. 8ff.

12. Gerhard von Rad, *Old Testament Theology*, vol. 1 (New York: Harper & Row, 1962), pp. 178ff.

13. Johannes Blauw, *The Missionary Nature of the Church: A Survey of the Biblical Theology of Mission* (Grand Rapids, Mich.: Wm. B. Eerdmans, 1974), p. 5.

14. Norman Habel, *Literary Criticism of the Old Testament* (Philadelphia: Fortress Press, 1971), pp. 48, 51.

15. Ernst Sellin and Georg Fohrer, *Introduction to the Old Testament* (Nashville: Abingdon Press, 1968), p. 178.

16. Walter A. Brueggemann, "Covenanting as Human Vocation: A Discussion of the Relation of the Bible and Pastoral Care," *Interpretation* 33.2 (April 1979), p. 123.

17. Walter A. Brueggemann, *The Prophetic Imagination* (Philadelphia: Fortress Press, 1978), pp. 62ff.

18. von Rad, *Old Testament Theology*, vol. 1, p. 354.

19. Gerhard von Rad, *Old Testament Theology*, vol. 2 (New York: Harper & Row, 1965), p. 137.

20. E. P. Sanders, *Paul and Palestinian Judaism: A Comparison* (Philadelphia: Fortress Press, 1977), p. 180.

21. Ibid., p. 549.

22. Ibid., pp. 85, 95, 119, 124.

23. Cushman, "Biblical Election," pp. 179ff. There is no better treatment available of the relevant scriptural texts on this theme, made all the more pertinent by Cushman's driving concern for the *oikoumenē* as the sphere of God's salvation.

24. See above, pp. 11f. Variously termed the "Apostolic Assembly," or the "Apostolic Council," this has been described as "the most important event in the history of the primitive church" (Günther Bornkamm, *Paul* [New York: Harper & Row, 1971], p. 31). It is beyond the scope of our study to enter into discussion over the term "apostle" and its authority in the church—something with which Paul wrestled throughout his ministry (ibid., pp. 18ff., 74ff.). It will be a premise of our remaining argument, however, that apostleship was an office peculiar to the early church, and was derived from Christ's direct resurrection commission (which Paul himself claimed from his Damascus Road experience [I Cor. 9:1-2, 15:8-9]). Our concern will rather be faithful discipleship as the mark of leadership for the church of today.

25. Robert L. Bellah, et al., *Habits of the Heart: Individualism and Commitment in American Life* (New York: Harper & Row, 1986), pp. 232ff.

26. It is salutary to refer to the exact wording of Schleiermacher's concept of the church, and to be reminded how Protestantism still labors under the weight of his terminology: "That a Church is nothing but a communion or association relating to religion or piety, is beyond all doubt for us Evangelical (Protestant) Christians, since we regard it as equivalent to degeneration in a Church when it begins to occupy itself with other matters as well . . .; just as we also always oppose any attempt on the part of the leaders of State or of science, as such, to order the affairs of religion . . . it is only the maintenance, regulation, and advancement of piety which they can regard as the essential business of the Church." Friedrich Schleiermacher, *The Christian Faith*, 2 vols. (New York: Harper & Row, 1963), 1:5f. See also Jürgen Moltmann, *Hope and Planning* (New York: Harper & Row, 1971), pp. 131ff.

27. Wolfhart Pannenberg, *Human Nature, Election, and History* (Philadelphia: Westminster Press, 1977), p. 82.

CHAPTER FOUR
THE CRITICAL JUDGMENT OF CHRIST

1. For a good introduction to these texts, see James M. Efird, *Revelation for Today: An Apocalyptic Approach* (Nashville: Abingdon Press, 1989).

2. The definitive historical account of these atrocities is by Martin Gilbert, *The Holocaust: A History of the Jews of Europe During the Second World War* (New York: Holt, Rinehart & Winston, 1985).

3. Hendrikus Boers, *Who Was Jesus? The Historical Jesus and the Synoptic Gospels* (San Francisco: Harper & Row, 1989), pp. 76ff.

4. See C. F. Evans, *Resurrection and the New Testament* (Naperville, Ill.: Alec

R. Allenson, 1970), pp. 14ff.; and Willi Marxsen, *The Resurrection of Jesus of Nazareth* (Philadelphia: Fortress Press, 1970), pp. 134ff. But see also Pinchas Lapide, *The Resurrection of Jesus: A Jewish Perspective* (Minneapolis: Augsburg Publishing House, 1983), pp. 60ff., where it is argued that the pre-Easter faith of the disciples, being influenced widely by the Pharisaism of the day, combined a certainty of a future resurrection of all with a possible earlier resurrection of some people especially graced by God (p. 64).

5. Richard R. Niebuhr, *Resurrection and Historical Reason* (New York: Charles Scribner's Sons, 1957), p. 29. See also Gerald O'Collins, *Jesus Risen: An Historical, Fundamental, and Systematic Examination of Christ's Resurrection* (New York: Paulist Press, 1987), pp. 99ff.

6. See Carl E. Braaten, *The Future of God: The Revolutionary Dynamics of Hope* (New York: Harper & Row, 1969), pp. 73ff.

7. Moltmann, *Theology of Hope*, pp. 186f.

8. Ibid., p. 148.

9. Albert C. Outler, "Canon Criticism and the Gospel of Mark," in *New Synoptic Studies: The Cambridge Conference and Beyond*, ed. William R. Farmer (Macon, Ga.: Mercer University Press, 1983), pp. 234f.

10. Leon Festinger, et al., *When Prophecy Fails* (Minneapolis: University of Minnesota Press, 1956).

11. William Styron, *Sophie's Choice* (New York: Bantam Books, 1980), p. 583.

12. I have reflected much on this insight since first hearing it articulated by Ruth Tiffany Barnhouse.

13. See Jürgen Moltmann, *The Crucified God: The Cross of Christ as the Foundation and Criticism of Christian Theology* (New York: Harper & Row, 1974), pp. 270ff.

14. Thus Anselm's theory of the Atonement. See Philip Schaff, *History of the Christian Church*, 8 vols. (Repr., Grand Rapids, Mich.: Wm. B. Eerdmans, 1980–84), 5:604f.

15. Above, p. 53. References in the following pages to *kairos, chronos, krisis,* and *aion* are drawn from the *Theological Dictionary of the New Testament*, ed. Gerhard Kittel and Gerhard Friedrich, tr. Geoffrey W. Bromiley, 10 vols. (Grand Rapids, Mich.: Wm. B. Eerdmans, 1965–76).

16. Hubert Cunliffe-Jones and Benjamin Drewery, eds., *A History of Christian Doctrine* (Philadelphia: Fortress Press, 1980), pp. 46ff.

17. González, *Christian Thought*, pp. 40ff.

18. Ibid., pp. 55f.

19. Benjamin Drewery, *Origen and the Doctrine of Grace* (London: Epworth Press, 1960), p. 156.

20. Ibid., p. 158.

21. Ibid., p. 130.

22. Robert Frost, "Snow," in *Mountain Interval* (New York: Henry Holt and Company, 1916), p. 84.

23. As, for example, in clause #15 of the Lausanne Covenant (1974). See Alfred C. Krass, *Evangelizing Neo-Pagan North America: The Word That Frees* (Scottdale, Pa.: Herald Press, 1982), pp. 196f.

24. Wesley, *Hymns*, pp. 324-25.

25. See above, pp. 16f.

26. On this, see Neuhaus, *Time Toward Home*, pp. 46ff.

27. Thus the title of William F. McElvaney's thought-provoking book, *Good News Is Bad News Is Good News* (Maryknoll, N.Y.: Orbis Books, 1980).

28. Carl E. Braaten, "The Meaning of Evangelism in the Context of God's Universal Grace," *Journal of the Academy for Evangelism in Theological Education*, vol. 3 (1987–1988), pp. 17f.

CHAPTER FIVE
SALVATION AND DISCIPLESHIP: A NECESSARY DISTINCTION

1. See above, pp. 15, 33, 37.

2. Robert E. Cushman, *Faith Seeking Understanding: Essays Theological and Critical* (Durham, N.C.: Duke University Press, 1981).

3. Ibid., p. xii.

4. Ibid., p. xiii.

5. Ibid., p. xiiif.

6. Ludwig Feuerbach, *Principles of the Philosophy of the Future* (New York: Bobbs-Merrill, 1966), p. 5.

7. See above, p. 69.

8. N. S. Tjernagel, *Henry VIII and the Lutherans: A Study in Anglo-Lutheran Relations from 1521–1547* (St. Louis: Concordia Publishing House, 1965), p. 19.

9. *Certain Sermons or Homilies Appointed to Be Read in Churches in the Time of Queen Elizabeth* (London: S.P.C.K., 1852), p. 20.

10. Ibid., pp. 32ff.

11. Ibid., p. 61.

12. The Synod held at Dort in 1618–19 took the following doctrinal positions: (T)otal human depravity; (U)nconditional election; (L)imited atonement; (I)rresistible grace; (P)erseverance of the elect.

13. John W. Packer, *The Transformation of Anglicanism 1643–60* (Manchester: Manchester University Press, 1969), p. 56.

14. *The Works of John Wesley: Volume 3: Sermons III*, ed. Albert C. Outler (Nashville: Abingdon Press, 1986), p. 207.

15. Cushman, *Faith*, p. 74.

16. Ibid., p. 73.

17. Wesley, *Hymns*, p. 82.

18. Meeks, *God the Economist*, p. 40.

19. See David Lowes Watson, "Prophetic Evangelism: The Good News of Global Grace," in *Wesleyan Theology Today: A Bicentennial Theological Consultation*, ed. Theodore Runyon (Nashville: Kingswood Books, Abingdon Press, 1985), pp. 219ff.

20. Oswald Chambers, *My Utmost for His Highest: Selections for the Year* (New York: Dodd, Mead & Co., 1935), p. 33.

21. See H. Eddie Fox and George E. Morris, *Faith-Sharing: Dynamic Christian Witnessing by Invitation* (Nashville: Discipleship Resources, 1986), for some creative alternatives to this common mistake in evangelism.

22. See above, p. 21.

23. See above, p. 22.

24. See David Lowes Watson, "Justification by Faith and Wesley's Evangelistic Message," *Wesleyan Theological Journal,* vol. 21, nos. 1 and 2 (Spring-Fall, 1986), pp. 7-23.

25. *The Journal of the Rev. John Wesley, A.M.,* standard ed., ed. Nehemiah Curnock, 8 vols. (London, 1909–1916), 2:349.

26. Ibid., 2:354ff.

27. Ibid., 2:356.

28. Ibid., 1:465ff.

29. Wesley, Sermons I, ed. Outler, pp. 450ff.

30. See esp. James W. Fowler, *Stages of Faith: The Psychology of Human Development and the Quest for Meaning* (San Francisco: Harper & Row, 1981).

31. Frank Whaling, ed., *John and Charles Wesley: Selected Writings and Hymns* (New York: Paulist Press, 1981), p. 140.

32. Herzog, *Liberation Theology,* p. 257.

CHAPTER SIX
CONGREGATIONS AND DISCIPLES: QUESTIONS OF IDENTITY

1. Juan Luis Segundo, *The Community Called Church* (Maryknoll, N.Y.: Orbis Books, 1973), p. 83. See also *The Hidden Motives of Pastoral Action* (Orbis, 1978), where Segundo provides a practical application of these ecclesiological principles, describing this line of least resistance as the "general rule of pastoral prudence . . . *the absolute minimum in obligations in order to keep the maximum number of people*" (p. 72).

2. Segundo, *Community Church,* p. 82.

3. Segundo, *Hidden Motives,* pp. 26ff.

4. See Juan Luis Segundo, *Faith and Ideologies* (Maryknoll, N.Y.: Orbis Books, 1984), pp. 71ff. See also pp. 123ff., where a clear distinction is drawn between the ideologies of self-projected religious values and living in the "values-structure" of God's coming reign—the necessary condition of true faith in God (cf. the Anglican *Homilies,* above, pp. 102ff.). In *God-Walk: Liberation Shaping Dogmatics* (Maryknoll, N.Y.: Orbis Books, 1988), Frederick Herzog presses the point further by emphasizing the divine initiative in all of this: "Faith is awakened conscience. This is 'knowledge of God.' . . . The core of the matter here is God's own activity, theo-praxis. As God continues to struggle for justice, the inner ear cannot help being touched by it. . . . So faith in its heart is this knowledge we have together with God. It is basically justice-knowledge" (pp. 67-68).

5. For example: Hans J. Margull, *Hope in Action: The Church's Task in the World* (Philadelphia: Muhlenberg Press, 1962); Isaac C. Rottenberg, *The Promise and the Presence: Toward a Theology of the Kingdom of God* (Grand Rapids, Mich.: Wm. B. Eerdmans, 1980); Carl E. Braaten, *The Apostolic Imperative: Nature and Aim of the Church's Mission and Ministry* (Minneapolis: Augsburg Publishing House, 1985). Other volumes already cited include: William J. Abraham, *The Logic of Evangelism;* Mortimer Arias, *Announcing the Reign of God;* Carl E. Braaten, *The Flaming Center;* Orlando E. Costas, *Christ Outside the Gate;*

J. C. Hoekendijk, *The Church Inside Out;* Alfred C. Krass, *Five Lanterns at Sundown.*

6. Richard Stoll Armstrong, *Faithful Witnesses: A Course in Evangelism for Presbyterian Laity* (Philadelphia: Geneva Press, 1987). These are resources of "New Age Dawning," the official evangelism program of the Presbyterian Church (U.S.A.).

7. Costas, *Christ Outside the Gate,* pp. 162ff.

8. Krass, *Evangelizing Neo-Pagan North America,* pp. 104ff.

9. This incisive turn of phrase comes from a conversation with Frederick Herzog, to whom I am deeply indebted for many such insights into contemporary Christian discipleship.

10. See, for example, Fred Smith, "The Mutuality of Evangelization: Father Inocente Salazar," in *Mission Trends No. 2: Evangelization,* ed. Gerald H. Anderson and Thomas F. Stransky, C.S.P. (New York: Paulist Press and Grand Rapids, Mich.: Wm. B. Eerdmans, 1975), pp. 139-44.

11. See Alexandre Ganoczy, "The Absolute Claim of Christianity: The Justification of Evangelization or an Obstacle to It?" in *Evangelization in the World Today,* ed. Norbert Greinacher and Alois Müller. Concilium #114 (New York: Seabury Press, 1979), pp. 23ff.

12. Above, pp. 65ff.

13. This phrase has had wide circulation in ecumenical dialogue. In addition to the title of the volume by Carl E. Braaten (above, p. 147, n. 10), see K. E. Skydsgaard, "The Flaming Center, or the Core of Tradition," in *Our Common History,* ed. John Deschner, et al., pp. 3-22 (above, pp. 147f., n. 3).

14. The role of both Protestant and Roman Catholic martyrs during the Reformation bears eloquent testimony to this. A more recent example, the Barmen Declaration of 1934, has already been cited (above, p. 27).

15. Robin Maas, *Crucified Love: The Practice of Christian Perfection* (Nashville: Abingdon Press, 1989), p. 49.

16. Mortimer Arias, *Announcing the Reign of God,* pp. 66f.

17. See, for example, Ray C. Petry, *Christian Eschatology and Social Thought* (Nashville: Abingdon Press, 1956), pp. 371ff.

18. For a helpful explanation of historiographical method in church history, see William A. Clebsch, *Christianity in European History* (New York: Oxford University Press, 1979), pp. 3-27.

19. See above, pp. 21ff.

20. See above, pp. 99ff.

21. John Foxe, *Actes and Monuments of These Latter and Perillous Dayes,* ed. Stephen Reed Cattley and George Townshend, 8 vols. (London: Seeley & Burnside, 1837–1841), 4:635.

22. See Lowell H. Zuck, ed., *Christianity and Revolution: Radical Christian Testimonies 1520–1650* (Philadelphia: Temple University Press, 1975).

23. *The Works of Gerrard Winstanley,* ed. George H. Sabine (Ithaca, N.Y.: Cornell University Press, 1941), p. 257.

24. See above, pp. 43ff.

25. *Works of Winstanley,* ed. Sabine, pp. 673-75.

26. Zuck, *Revolution,* p. 244.

27. Gerald R. Cragg, *Puritanism in the Period of the Great Persecution 1660–1688* (Cambridge: University Press, 1957).

28. For example: Norman Cohn, *The Pursuit of the Millennium: Revolutionary Millenarians and Mystical Anarchists of the Middle Ages* (New York: Oxford University Press, 1970); Rosemary Radford Ruether, *The Radical Kingdom: The Western Expansion of Messianic Hope* (New York: Harper & Row, 1970).

29. K. James Stein, *Philipp Jakob Spener: Pietist Patriarch* (Chicago: Covenant Press, 1986), p. 88.

30. For example, E. P. Thompson, *The Making of the English Working Class* (New York: Vintage Books, 1966), pp. 350ff.

31. *The Works of John Wesley: Volume 9: The Methodist Societies: History, Nature, and Design*, ed. Rupert E. Davies (Nashville: Abingdon Press, 1989), pp. 69-73.

32. See, for example, *The Letters of John Wesley*, ed. John Telford, 8 vols. (London: Epworth Press, 1931), 4:194. See also Robert E. Cushman, *John Wesley's Experimental Divinity: Studies in Methodist Doctrinal Standards* (Nashville: Kingswood Books, 1989), p. 140.

33. *The Works of John Wesley: Volume 3: Sermons III*, ed. Albert C. Outler (Nashville: Abingdon Press, 1986), pp. 58-69.

34. Stein, *Spener*, p. 90.

35. David Lowes Watson, *The Early Methodist Class Meeting: Its Origins and Significance* (Nashville: Discipleship Resources, 1985), pp. 70ff.

36. *The Lives of Early Methodist Preachers, Chiefly Written by Themselves*, ed. Thomas Jackson, 6th ed. (London: Wesleyan Conference Office, 1873).

37. Donald W. Dayton, *Discovering an Evangelical Heritage* (New York: Harper & Row, 1976).

38. See Robert McAfee Brown, *Spirituality and Liberation: Overcoming the Great Fallacy* (Philadelphia: Westminster Press, 1988).

39. Guillermo Cook, *The Expectation of the Poor: Latin American Base Ecclesial Communities in Protestant Perspective* (Maryknoll, N.Y.: Orbis Books, 1985), p. 61. See also Alvaro Barreiro, *Basic Ecclesial Communities: The Evangelization of the Poor* (Maryknoll, N.Y.: Orbis Books, 1982), and Dominique Barbé, *Grace and Power: Base Communities and Nonviolence in Brazil* (Maryknoll, N.Y.: Orbis Books, 1987).

40. Cook, *Expectation*, p. 64.

41. Ibid., pp. 89ff.

42. Ibid., p. 68.

43. Juan Luis Segundo, *The Liberation of Theology* (Maryknoll, N.Y.: Orbis Books, 1976), p. 9.

44. Gustavo Gutiérrez, *We Drink from Our Own Wells: The Spiritual Journey of a People* (Maryknoll, N.Y.: Orbis Books, 1984), p. 72.

45. Leonardo Boff, *Ecclesiogenesis: The Base Communities Reinvent the Church* (Maryknoll, N.Y.: Orbis Books, 1986).

46. Ibid., p. 60.

47. Ibid. See also pp. 37ff.

48. In posing these questions, it is important to remember that the United States of America is a comparatively well-churched and Christianized culture; which is why reforming ecclesial movements in other countries can rarely be used as direct paradigms for the North American church. Thus, for example, the house church model (see Del Birkey, *The House Church: A Model for*

Renewing the Church [Scottdale, Pa.: Herald Press, 1988]), or the home cell group (see Paul Yonggi Cho, with Harold Hostetler, *Successful Home Cell Groups* [South Plainfield, N.J.: Bridge Publishing Co., 1981]), though offering helpful insights into more intentional Christian discipleship, must always be carefully adapted to the predominantly congregational pattern of North American churchly life. This is likewise true of the *comunidades de base*, used as a case study in this chapter. Not only is it difficult to relate a Latin American grassroots movement to the socioeconomic realities of the United States (though there are exceptions, such as the inner cities of the nation), but there is also the further reality of a predominantly Protestant North American ecclesial culture (see Cook, *Expectation,* pp. 200ff.).

For an interesting overview of contemporary renewal in the North American church, including some examples of crosscultural adaptation, see Richard B. Wilke, *Signs and Wonders: The Mighty Work of God in the Church* (Nashville: Abingdon Press, 1989). See also David W. Shenk and Ervin R. Stutzman, *Creating Communities of the Kingdom: New Testament Models of Church Planting* (Scottdale, Pa.: Herald Press, 1988); and Robert Banks, *Paul's Idea of Community: The Early House Churches in Their Historical Setting* (Grand Rapids, Mich.: Wm. B. Eerdmans, 1980).

49. See Victor Turner, *The Ritual Process* (Chicago: Aldine Publishing Co., 1969), pp. 131-65.

CONCLUSION
CHRIST-CENTERED CONGREGATIONS

1. See above, pp. 113f.

2. James D. Anderson and Ezra Earl Jones, *The Management of Ministry* (San Francisco: Harper & Row, 1978), chap. 6. See esp. pp. 124ff.

3. All these examples are of necessity a minimal representation of such movements and groupings. The fact that in many instances the cutting edge of God's coming *shalom* is not to be found in congregational life *per se* makes the conclusion of our study inescapable: that disciplined disciples must be acknowledged as congregational leaders; and that we must make this acknowledgment with utmost urgency.

4. Walter H. Capps, *Time Invades the Cathedral: Tensions in the School of Hope* (Philadelphia: Fortress Press, 1972), p. 3.

5. Frederick Herzog, *God-Walk*, pp. 168ff.

6. Michael H. Crosby, *Disciples*, pp. 53, 80f., 89ff.

I N D E X

Abraham, William J., 52
American Revolution, as analogy of salvation and discipleship, 16-17, 92ff.
Amnesty International, 143
Amphetamines. *See* Spiritual amphetamines
Anderson, James D., 148
Apostolic Conference, 11, 69-70, 98, 151
Arias, Mortimer, 64

Balch, David L., 50
Barmen Declaration, 27
Barrett, David B., 24
Base Ecclesial Communities, 131ff., 143
Beelzebul, as ruler of present worldly powers, 41, 62-63
Bilney, Thomas, 125
Boff, Leonardo, 10, 133-34
Bonhoeffer, Dietrich, 26-27
Braaten, Carl E., 14, 94

Carter, Jimmy, 22-23
Chambers, Oswald, 108
Christ. *See* Jesus Christ
Christian discipleship, disciples: authority of, 41-42; balance in, 128ff.; childlike trust of, 19; Christ-centeredness of, 104-5; cost of, 20, 29-30; diffidence of in North American church, 109-10; in early church, 49ff.; as family of God, 42; invitation to, 108; leaders in, 145-46; in Matthew's Gospel, 40ff.; meaning of, 19ff., 39ff.; obligations of, 22ff.; origins of, 38ff.; particularity of, 57-58; point of, 93-94; privatization of, 104;

radical nature of, 120ff., 143-44; rejection of by the church, 122; and relationship with Christ, 39ff., 47ff., 104; and relationship with the church, 120ff.; and righteousness of God, 42ff.; and salvation, 55, 106ff., 137-38; semantic slippage in defining, 21; and surrender to God, 48-49; tensions caused by, 120ff., 143-44; of the Twelve, 39ff.
Church: and base ecclesial communities, 133ff.; blockage of grace in, 12-13; centripetal inertia of, 12, 23-24; Christ-centeredness of, 142ff.; and culture, 10; identity of, 15-16, 37, 105, 115ff., 119ff., 137; as justified by Christ, 144-45; membership in, 21-22, 29; as messengers of the gospel, 9, 56-57; in North America, 9, 12, 15, 35ff.; renewal movements in, 121ff.; as resident aliens, 16; as servant, 9; as sign community, 116-17; as true patriots, 16; universal commission of, 10, 57-58, 69; as visible community, 35; wide range of ministry in, 140ff. *See also Ecclesiolae in Ecclesia; Ekklēsia*
Clergy, role of the, 24ff., 145-46
Consumerism, 29
Conversion. *See* Repentance and conversion
Cook, Guillermo, 131-33
Costas, Orlando E., 25
Covenant with God: of Israel, 67-68; new covenant in Christ, 68-69; obedience as condition of, 67-68
Cragg, Gerald R., 127
Cranmer, Thomas, 103

158